MICHELE ARNOLD

40 DAYS OF PRAYER
FOR YOUR HUSBAND

In His Grace Ministries LLC

THE JOURNEY

Copyright © 2020 Michele Arnold. All rights reserved.

Cover photograph and author photograph by Jarod Arnold. Copyright © 2020 All rights reserved.

THE HOLY BIBLE, NEW INTERNATIONAL VERSION®, NIV® Copyright © 1973, 1978, 1984, 2011 by Biblica, Inc.® Used by permission. All rights reserved worldwide.

Unless otherwise indicated, all Scripture quotations are taken from the Holy Bible, New Living Translation, copyright © 1996, 2004, 2015 by Tyndale House Foundation. Used by permission of Tyndale House Publishers, Inc., Carol Stream, Illinois 60188. All rights reserved.

Scripture taken from the NEW AMERICAN STANDARD BIBLE®, Copyright © 1960,1962,1963,1968,1971,1972,1973,1975,1977,1995 by The Lockman Foundation. Used by permission.

Scripture taken from the New King James Version®. Copyright © 1982 by Thomas Nelson. Used by permission. All rights reserved.

All rights reserved. No part of this publication may be reproduced, stored in a retrieval system or transmitted in any form or by any means, electronic, mechanical, photocopying, recording or otherwise without the prior permission of the publisher or in accordance with the provisions of the Copyright, Designs and Patents Act 1988 or under the terms of any license permitting limited copying issued by the Copyright Licensing Agency.

ISBN - 978-1-7351373-6-0

Published by In His Grace Ministries LLC

Book website
www.inhisgrace.com/product/the-journey/

Dedication

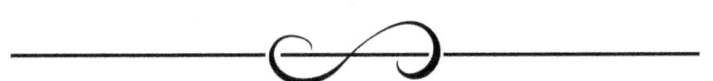

To my daughter. This devotional was birthed out of unfortunate and painful circumstances in your life. Circumstances where I wanted to speak truth, love, and peace into. I found a letter I wrote to you in 2012 when you were 17 years old. I found it very fitting as my introduction to your book, your devotional. I am so proud of you and all that you have accomplished. Keep God in the center of your life and remember who He says that you are. I love you!

To my son, who diligently worked with me on creating the best cover and author photo I could ask for. You spent time with me, listening to my vision and retaking photo after photo to capture what my vision was. I thank you so very much. I am proud of you, and I am excited to see where you are heading with your photography. I love you!

To my husband, thank you for your constant encouragement, support, and editing skills. And thank you for being there to bounce ideas off of and for praying over me throughout this process. I am so thankful to be doing life with you and so excited to see where God is taking us.
I love you!

To my friends and family, thank you for your never-ending love and support. I love you!

Contents

Introduction 1
Wife - Who I am 5
Identity/Purpose 13
Walk with the Lord 19
Health 25
Discernment 33
Wisdom 39
Marriage 43
Future 49
Wife – Submission 55
Worship 61
Heart 67
Mind 73
Insecurities 77
Past 81
Strongholds 87
Husband 93
Wife – Equal 99
Prayer 105
Fruit 109
Friendship 115

Contents

Strength/Courage 121
Kindness 127
Forgiveness 133
Intimacy 141
Wife – Serve 147
Father 153
Leading his family 161
Job 167
Finances 173
Fear 181
Peace/Hope 187
Protection 193
Wife – Respect 199
Integrity 205
Words/Speech 211
Honesty 217
Trust 221
Priorities 227
Attitude 235
Temptations 239

Introduction

The following letter to my daughter is full of spelling, grammatical, and literary errors. However, to maintain authenticity of the letter itself, I have left it as is.

My darling daughter,

    I know that you may not be in the right place right now to really hear what I am going to say. I just hope that you will at least take the time to read and pray over what I am saying. I love you so very much and I only want what is best for you. Entering into a boyfriend/girlfriend or marriage relationship must be done with both eyes wide open and to remember that your husband will not be everything that you need. That your relationship with Christ is the only one that will fulfill your every need and is the most important relationship you will ever have. Your relationship with Christ is to be held above all else. If you don't mind I will write to you multiple letters on what to look for in a husband. Because we all know that when you date someone it typically is not just for fun but in many ways courting. Finding out if this particular person is the right one for me. Is this the person that God has set aside just for me.

    A husband should be many things, loving, caring, confident, honest, a man after God's own heart and the list can go on and on. I would like to touch upon a few of the key traits that you should be looking for and aware of in your search for a husband.

    As we grow and look to find a husband a woman's first reaction is are they good looking, are they sweet, how do I feel when I think of them, when I look at them and how they make me feel when they talk to me or when they touch me. These are all fine and good but that is only scratching the surface of where to begin. Love is more than a feeling, Love is an action…… *"Love is patient, love is kind, it does not envy, it does not boast, it is not proud. It does not dishonor others, it is not self-seeking, it is not easily angered, it keeps no record of wrongs. Love does not delight in evil, but rejoices with the truth. It always protects, always trusts, always hopes and always perseveres."* 1 Corinthians 13:4-7 (NIV)

First and for most he should love Jesus. Be a man after God's own heart. To have a personal relationship with Christ. To be someone who is not afraid to stand up for what he believes in even if it is unpopular with todays culture. To pray and seek God's guidance in their life, to always find God in everything that he does.

Love can show up in many many different ways. From big to small gestures. For example: To allow the young man the opportunity to open a door for you. Knowing that you are a strong independent young woman to allow a man to open a door for you is not diminishing who you are at all. Better yet you are allowing in some small way for this young man to fulfill part of who he is as a man. The part that is there to take care of and to serve his wife/girlfriend. A man who is willing to clear the dishes for you after a meal, to rub your back when you are having a bad day or even if your day was one of the best. To serve you with faithfulness and love. No complaints and no tallies as to who has done more for the other. A willingness and an openness to put himself out there for you and you alone.

To witness and see the life that he leads not just with you but others around him. How he treats those closest to him and those who are not. How he speaks to his father and mother, his best friends and those all around him. He is a leader not only in your relationship but in the rest of his life as well. In school, with his friends at his job. He graciously and gently guides those he is put in "charge of". To lead with a firm but gentle hand and to wisely heed the counsel of those above him and those who have great influence over him.

Consider greatly and prayerfully before entering into any relationship. As God will always guide you to the right person. Our heart can sometimes deceive us and we have to tune into Christ and listen closely to what it is that He is saying in our lives and the places that He is guiding us. If you listen and obey things will fall into place. Be where they ought to be and flow where they ought to flow. *"Come near to God and He will come near to you"* ~ James 4:8 (NIV)

Day 1
Wife - Who I am

"A wife of noble character who can find?"
Proverbs 31:10 (NIV)

A wife of noble character who can find? What does a wife of noble character look like, who is she really, and what do I do once I find out? Proverbs 31 gives us a list of characteristics of what a Godly woman looks like.

She is:

Trustworthy
"An excellent wife who can find? For her worth is far above jewels. The heart of her husband trusts in her, and he will have no lack of gain. She does him good, and not evil, all the days of her life."
Verse 10-12 (NASB)

Works hard and is not lazy
She selects wool and flax and works with eager hands."
Verse 13 (NIV)

"She rises also while it is still night and gives food to her household"
Verse 15 (NASB)

"She sets about her work vigorously; her arms are strong for her tasks."
Verse 17 (NIV)

"In her hand she holds the distaff and grasps the spindle with her fingers"
Verse 19 (NIV)

"She looks well to the ways of her household, and does not eat the bread of idleness."
Verse 27 (NASB)

<u>Intelligent, business savvy</u>
"She considers a field and buys it; from her earnings she plants a vineyard."
Verse 16 (NASB)

"She sees that her trading is profitable, and her lamp does not go out at night."
Verse 18 (NIV)

"She makes linen garments and sells them, and supplies the merchants with sashes."
Verse 24 (NIV)

<u>Charitable</u>
"She opens her arms to the poor and extends her hands to the needy."
Verse 20 (NIV)

<u>Does not fear</u>
"She is not afraid of the snow for her household, for all her household are clothed with scarlet"
Verse 21 (NASB)

<u>Clothed in strength and dignity</u>
"She is clothed with strength and dignity, and she laughs without fear of the future"
Verse 25 (NLT)

<u>Wise</u>
"She speaks with wisdom, and faithful instruction is on her tongue."
Verse 26 (NIV)

Respected
"Her children arise and call her blessed; her husband also, and he praises her: "Many women do noble things, but you surpass them all."
Verse 28-29 (NIV)

Caregiver
"She is like merchant ships; she brings her food from afar."
Verse 14 (NASB)

"She makes coverings for bed; she is clothed in fine linen and purple."
Verse 22 (NIV)

Fears the Lord
"Charm is deceitful, and beauty is vain, but a woman who fears the Lord, she shall be praised."
Verse 30 (NASB)

So how do we develop these characteristics? We start from within. We remember who God says we are. We position ourselves in God's Word and imitate who He is.

"Follow my example as I follow the example of Christ" 1 Corinthians 11:1 (NIV)

"Therefore be imitators of God, as beloved children; and walk in love, just as Christ also loved you and gave Himself up for us, an offering and sacrifice to God as a fragrant aroma." Ephesians 5:1-2 (NASB)

"the one who says he abides in Him ought himself to walk in the same manner as He walked." 1 John 2:6 (NASB)

You strive and drive to be the best version that God created you to be. You work hard. You continue to learn. You are generous to others. You are loving, kind, and trustworthy in all things. You never want to compare yourself to anyone else. We are to only measure ourselves against Christ *"Each one should test their own actions. Then they can take pride in themselves alone, without comparing themselves to someone else, for each one should carry their own load"* Galatians 6:4-5 (NIV)

The most important thing to remember is who God is. He is the Great I AM—The Alpha and Omega, the beginning and the end. He is love; He is grace, and He is mercy. He is always present. Miracle worker, creator of the world. Our Savior. Our peace. Our hope. He is our Father.

Once we understand our place with the Lord, we will understand our role as a wife much better. Who does God say that I am? Who does God say that you are?

In the midst of knowing who God is, we remember who we are. I call these the "I am's". Who God says I am. You are loved. You are cherished. You are valued. You are known. You are protected. You are chosen. You are blessed, confident, His friend, and His masterpiece. You are fearfully and wonderfully made. You are the daughter of a KING!

<u>I am a daughter of the King</u>
"So in Christ Jesus you are all children of God through faith"
Galatians 3:26 (NIV)

<u>His special possession</u>
"But you are a chosen people, a royal priesthood, a holy nation, God's special possession, that you may declare the praises of Him who called you out of darkness into His wonderful light."
1 Peter 2:9 (NIV)

<u>Renewed</u>
"Do not lie to each other, since you have taken off your old self with its practices and have put on the new self, which is being renewed in knowledge in the image of its Creator."
Colossians 3:9-10 (NIV)

<u>Loved</u>
"Give thanks to the God of Heaven. His love endures forever."
Psalm 136:26 (NIV)

"and hope does not disappoint, because the love of God has been poured out within our hearts through the Holy Spirit who was given to us."
Romans 5:5 (NASB)

<u>Workmanship</u>
"For we are his workmanship, created in Christ Jesus for good works, which God prepared beforehand, so that we would walk in them."
Ephesians 2:10 (NASB)

<u>Holy (set apart for God)</u>
"because it is written, "You shall be holy, for I am holy.""
1 Peter 1:16 (NASB)

<u>I am complete</u>
"and in Christ you have been brought to fullness. He is the head over every power and authority."
Colossians 2:10 (NIV)

<u>At peace</u>
"And the peace of God, which transcends all understanding, will guard your hearts and your minds in Christ Jesus."
Philippians 4.7 (NIV)

<u>Fearfully and wonderfully made</u>
"I will give thanks to You, for I am fearfully and wonderfully made; Wonderful are your works, and my soul knows it very well."
Psalm 139:14 (NASB)

My self-worth, and your self-worth, is not wrapped up in being a wife, a mother, a daughter, a sister, or a friend. Self-worth is set in who God says that you are. I encourage you to write out these verses. Place them on your bathroom mirror, on your refrigerator, above the TV, in your car, on your phone, and anywhere else you can think of, so you can meditate (filling your mind) on these things.

Now that we have established who we are in Christ, we can then move on to who we are as a wife. What does this look like? How am I to act, whether in good times or in bad times? We will find out how in further chapters on being a wife.

Prayer

Dear Lord,

      Heavenly Father, I come to you today, asking for your hand over my life and the life of my husband. Before I can learn to be a wife, I have to learn who I am in You. Help me cling to what Your Word says about who I am. I am loved, Holy, set apart for You, and at peace. I am Your prized possession. I am complete in You and Your workmanship. I am fearfully and wonderfully made. Help me be the wife you have created me to be. Help me look to your Word to learn and to grow and to follow Jesus' example by taking pride in myself and my accomplishments. I ask you, Lord, to help position me in your Word so I can gain knowledge and understanding of who You are and who I am supposed to be. I praise You and I thank You, in Your precious name, because You meet us where we are at. You gave up Your life because You loved us. You offered us hope, grace, mercy, and love. You redeemed us for the purpose of loving others. I pray. Amen.

Notes

My Prayer

Day 2
Identity/Purpose

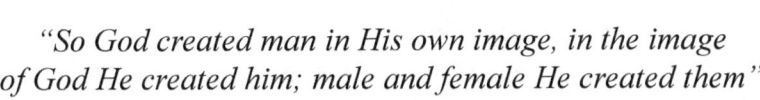

"So God created man in His own image, in the image of God He created him; male and female He created them"
Genesis 1:27 (NKJV)

Sometimes it can be a struggle for your husband to not wrap his job, his hobbies, and his friends up into his identity. We have to go to the Scriptures to help our husbands identify who they are.

Your husband, if a believer, is a child of God *"Yet to all who did receive him, to those who believed in his name, He gave the right to become children of God"* John 1:12 (NIV), who is loved beyond measure. He is created in God's image, a masterpiece that is sculpted by His hands. He is set apart and appointed. Your husband is God's special possession. *"For I know the plans I have for you," declares the Lord, "plans to prosper you and not to harm you, plans to give you a hope and a future."* Jeremiah 29:11 (NIV) You need to remind your husband and yourself of these truths daily. Speak them over your husband so he doesn't forget them. We forget sometimes that our worth is not wrapped up in others and what we do. But rather our worth is wrapped up in God and God alone. Our identity is wrapped up in who God says we are.

God's Image
"So God created mankind in His own image, in the image of God He created them; male and female He created them."
Genesis 1:27 (NIV)

God's Masterpiece
"For we are God's masterpiece. He has created us anew in Christ Jesus, so we can do the good things He planned for us long ago."
Ephesians 2:10 (NLT)

The world doesn't need to know my name.
because He knows my name.

I don't need to stand tall before men
because I kneel at the feet of Jesus.

What others think of me does not matter.
because God knows my heart.

I don't need to be accepted and loved by the world.
because I am accepted and loved by God.

The world can throw as many "stones" as they want at me.
With the strength that God provides, I will pick myself up and return into the "city".

If threats abound, I will not fear for God gave me a spirit, not of fear but of power, love and self-control.

I will not give up when it's hard.
I press on toward the goal to win the prize to which God in Christ Jesus is calling us upward.

The Armor of God

"Finally, be strong in the Lord and in his mighty power. Put on the full armor of God, so that you can take your stand against the devil's schemes. For our struggle is not against flesh and blood, but against the rulers, against the authorities, against the powers of this dark world and against the spiritual forces of evil in the heavenly realms. Therefore put on the full armor of God, so that when the day of evil comes, you may be able to stand your ground, and after you have done everything, to stand. Stand firm then, with the belt of truth buckled around your waist, with the breastplate of righteousness in place, and with your feet fitted with the readiness that comes from the gospel of peace. In addition to all this, take up the shield of faith, with which you can extinguish all the flaming arrows of the evil one. Take the helmet of salvation and the sword of the Spirit, which is the word of God. And pray in the Spirit on all occasions with all kinds of

prayers and requests. With this in mind, be alert and always keep on praying for all the Lord's people." Ephesians 6:10-18 (NIV)

Prayer

Dear Lord,

     Our identity and purpose should stem from You and You alone. I pray that my husband finds his identity in You and seeks You in all things. When the world comes at him, and it will, I pray that he would be able to see himself in You. May his whole being be rooted in who You say that He is, Your special possession, Your masterpiece, and so much more. I ask that he is able to take on who You say that he is and move forward with a newfound confidence in himself. In Your name Lord, I pray. Amen.

Notes

My Prayer

Day 3
Walk with the Lord

"Therefore, as you received Christ Jesus the Lord, so walk in Him"
Colossians 2:6 (NASB)

What should our walk with the Lord look like? The Scriptures tell us they will know us for our fruit.

"But the fruit of the Spirit is love, joy, peace, patience, kindness, goodness, faithfulness, gentleness, self-control; against such things there is no law."
Galatians 5:22-23 (NASB)

As we grow closer to the Lord, the fruits of the Spirit will start to come naturally to us. We, of course, stumble and fall from time to time. We won't always show up like we should. Why? Even though I'm right with God?

Because *"for all have sinned and fall short of the glory of God."* Romans 3:23 (NIV) None of us are perfect, but we follow the perfect example, Jesus.

We see many times where Jesus made it a priority to spend time in prayer. He spent time alone with the Father. If Jesus, being one with the Father, knew the importance of spending time with the Father, shouldn't we?

Life gets busy, and life gets messy, but we can't forget or ignore our time with our Heavenly Father. We are told repeatedly that we will have trials in this world, but we are to take joy within them. We are to cling to the Father for His comfort and peace. He is our pathway in times such as these.

Time spent with Him, being knowledgeable in the Word and being doers of the Word, is all very important to our walk with the Lord. We are to hide the Word in our hearts, so we can easily fall back on it, and so we can praise God during our joyous times and our sorrowful times.

The Bible comes in many different translations. The most common are the New American Standard Bible (NASB), English Standard Version (ESV), New International Version (NIV), New Living Translation (NLT), and King James Version (KJV).

Find the translation that is easy for you to follow and understand. A great resource is BibleGateway.com. You can search by verse or keywords, look up commentary, and do so much more. But the one thing I find most helpful is the comparison option. Here you can compare and contrast different translations side by side.

One of the best commentary sites I have found is called Enduring Word. The site guides you verse by verse through the Scriptures, giving you a better grasp and understanding of what you are reading. You can gain historical and cultural background within the text which is so important. All of these help you better understand the context within which the Bible was written.

Find the perfect spot to spend your quiet time with the Lord. This can be multiple places, or it can just be one. For me, it is one of four places. Of the four, my most favorite places are in my office and on our sunporch. It doesn't matter where your preferred spot is as long as you find the time to do it.

Our walk with the Lord is not just something we do on Sundays or in the privacy of our own homes. It also encompasses being out in public, at our jobs, with our friends, and how we interact and respond to one another. Who we hang out with, our friends, our inner circle, and the people we choose to surround ourselves with matters. The people who we hold close have a huge impact on our lives and on our daily walk with the Lord. Our walk with the Lord encompasses all those things and more. But our walk is also very personal and intimate, and it should continually be growing.

Figure out what works best for you and for your husband. Encourage one another and be accountable to one another in your walk with the Lord. If you journal, then include this into your quiet time. If you are a note taker, have a paper and pen handy or a tablet. Make sure you do not become distracted if you use one of these tools. Make sure you walk with God on a daily basis. Your faith and your trust in God won't grow without time spent with Him.

Prayer

Dear Lord,

I know and understand that time spent with you is so imperative to my walk. I ask that my husband would also understand the importance of his walk with You. I pray that he would take this on seriously and earnestly. May he gather around him the tools and the people needed to grow deeper in love with You and grow deeper in his knowledge and understanding of the Scriptures. I pray that he would hide Your Scriptures on the tablets of his heart to reference back to when needed. In Your name, I pray. Amen.

Notes

My Prayer

Day 4
Health

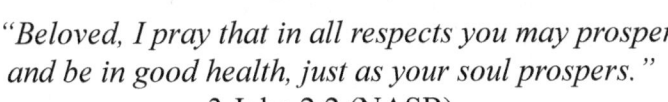

"Beloved, I pray that in all respects you may prosper and be in good health, just as your soul prospers."
3 John 2:2 (NASB)

When we think about heath, we tend to think about the physical and mental aspects and can forget the spiritual health of our husbands. Yes, their mental and physical health, as well as yours, are very important. Eating healthy, splurging every once in a while, and staying fit are all things we need to do. However, if our physical health fails us, our spiritual health takes over and ensures our place in the new heavens and the new earth.

Let's briefly talk about our physical health for a moment. It's interesting and intriguing how God made the body to work. He sets things up internally to alert us of things that may be going on. For example, pain is a trigger to our brains to alert us that something could potentially be wrong. But what I find fascinating is that God uses, at times, physical ailments to tell us that our actions, our thoughts, and our feelings are wrong. Let me explain.

Let's take a look at the life of David. He wrote many of the Psalms, some directly relating to his sin with Bathsheba, some when he was being pursued by his enemies, and some where David's unrepentant sin causes physical ailments within him.

Some scholars believe that Psalm 32 is interconnected to David's unrepentant sin with Bathsheba, which he laments in Psalms 51 before his friend Nathan confronted him and he confessed to his sins.

"Blessed is the one whose transgressions are forgiven, whose sins are

covered. Blessed is the one whose sin the Lord does not count against them and in whose spirit is no deceit. When I kept silent, my bones wasted away through my groaning all day long. For day and night your hand was heavy on me; my strength was sapped as in the heat of summer. Then I acknowledged my sin to you and did not cover up my iniquity. I said, "I will confess my transgressions to the Lord." And you forgave the guilt of my sin." Psalm 32:1-5 (NIV)

We witness another example of how unrepented sin directly affects our physical wellbeing.

"Because of your wrath there is no health in my body; there is no soundness in my bones because of my sin. My guilt has overwhelmed me like a burden too heavy to bear. My wounds fester and are loathsome because of my sinful folly. I am bowed down and brought very low; all day long I go about mourning. My back is filled with searing pain; there is no health in my body. I am feeble and utterly crushed; I groan in anguish of heart. All my longings lie open before you, Lord; my sighing is not hidden from you. My heart pounds, my strength fails me; even the light has gone from my eyes." Psalm 38:3-10 (NIV)

There is a real physical change in a person when they sin and don't ask for forgiveness or repent before the Lord. It is a weight upon their shoulders. They start to look different, and the life in their eyes is now gone. I have seen this firsthand. Someone dear to me had a sin so deep it affected their day to day. It affected their physical wellbeing. Their appearance even changed. All of this was because they were hiding their sin, and not yet ready to give it up. Then, one day, the Lord got a hold of their heart. The physical alignments they were suffering from all but seemed to disappear. The life returned to their eyes, and I could see the peace of God return to their soul and happiness found its way back in.

Some, if not most people, tend to believe that our physical ailments are just that, physical. Physical ailments have no rhyme or reason. Now, this can be true, but it is also true that our sin, or the sins of others, carries so much more weight than we realize. This isn't to say that every time we get sick, or have an injury, etc., that it is due to unrepentant sin. If we get sick, it doesn't mean that we didn't pray hard enough or good enough because sometimes we just get sick. Sometimes, we have a genetic disorder. Sometimes we get cancer. It just means that a deep-seated, deep-rooted sin such as David's can have a very real, and very physical, mental, and emotional effect on a person.

If our spiritual walk is healthy, then it will be easier to deal with our physical, mental, and emotional health. So how do we take care of our spiritual health?

Spend time with God. As with any relationship, you need to spend time with them.

"But seek first the kingdom of God and His righteousness, and all these things shall be added to you." Matthew 6:33 (NKJV

Read your Bible. Get to know what God's Word says.

"I have hidden your word in my heart that I might not sin against you." Psalm 119:11 (NLT)

Pray. This is how you talk with God. Pray about what is on your heart and seek His wisdom, His will, and His Word.

"Now it came to pass in those days that He went out to the mountain to pray, and continued all night in prayer to God." Luke 6:12 (NKJV)

Spend time with other Bible believing people. Who you choose to spend your time with will affect your day to day.

"Do not be deceived: "Bad company corrupts good morals." 1 Corinthians 15:33 (NASB)

Attend church. Find a church where they teach Scripture, and where you can get plugged in and serve. Be a part of the 20%, meaning that 80% of the work that needs to be done in a church is typically done by 20% of the people. Be doers of the Word, not just consumers.

"And let us consider one another in order to stir up love and good works,

not forsaking the assembling of ourselves together, as is the manner of some, but exhorting one another, and so much the more as you see the Day approaching." Hebrews 10:24-25 (NKJV)

Serve in the church, in wherever God calls you or there is need. Serve your friends and those in need.

"Each of you should use whatever gift you have received to serve others, as faithful stewards of God's grace in its various forms." 1 Peter 4:10 (NIV)

Maintain good health. We do this by what we eat, when we exercise, and how we treat our bodies.

"Or do you not know that your body is a temple of the Holy Spirit who is in you, whom you have from God, and that you are not your own? For you have been bought with a price: therefore glorify God in your body." 1 Corinthians 6:19-20 (NASB)

There are verses in the Scriptures that speak to our physical, mental, emotional and spiritual health. I will leave you with a few to meditate on.

<u>Physical health</u>
"for bodily discipline is only of little profit, but godliness is profitable for all things, since it holds promise for the present life and also for the life to come." 1 Timothy 4:8 (NASB)

<u>Mental health</u>
"I am leaving you with a gift—peace of mind and heart. And the peace I give is a gift the world cannot give. So don't be troubled or afraid."
John 14:27 (NLT)

" Be anxious for nothing, but in everything by prayer and supplication, with thanksgiving, let your requests be made known to God; and the peace of God, which surpasses all understanding, will guard your hearts and minds through Christ Jesus."
Philippians 4:6-7 (NKJV)

"casting all your anxiety on Him because He cares for you."
1 Peter 5:7 (NASB)

Emotional health
"A joyful heart is good medicine, but a broken spirit dries up the bones."
Proverbs 17:22 (NASB)

"A heart at peace gives life to the body, but envy rots the bones."
Proverbs 14:30 (NIV)

Spiritual health
"Beloved, I pray that you may prosper in all things and be in health, just as your soul prospers."
3 John 1:2 (NKJV)

"Then Jesus said to His disciples, "If anyone desires to come after Me, let him deny himself, and take up his cross, and follow Me."
Matthew 16:24 (NKJV)

Prayer

Dear Lord,

I pray not only for the physical, mental, and emotional health of my husband, but for his spiritual health as well. I ask that he would be strong for the tasks that lay before him, and that he would be mentally ready for anything that may come his way. I ask that his emotional health would be where it needs to be. But Lord, I want to focus on my husband's spiritual health. Give him a heart for You, so he would be in Your Word daily, surround himself with Godly friends, and find a church family to serve and be a part of. If his spiritual health is where it needs to be, we will be better prepared to handle the other aspects of health. We love you, Lord, and we pray in Your name, Lord. Amen.

Notes

My Prayer

Day 5
Discernment

"And this is my prayer: that your love may abound more and more in knowledge and depth of insight, so that you may be able to discern what is best and may be pure and blameless for the day of Christ"
Philippians 1:9-10 (NIV)

Recently, I had a friend lovingly and gently address with me what she felt might create bitterness in my life.

She said the following: *"For if you forgive other people when they sin against you, your heavenly Father will also forgive you. But if you do not forgive others their sins, your Father will not forgive your sins."* Matthew 6:14-15 (NIV)

I praise God for your friendship! I am so thankful for you and the way you live by your heart your love is deep and fierce.

It saddens me to know that your heart is hurting and for justifiable reasons! And out of concern for you my sweet friend I beg you to examine your heart and pluck out any seeds of bitterness or hate or anger. I plead with you to seek the Holy Spirit's guidance in identifying any stronghold so that you may get rid of it in its entirety and free yourself from its heaviness" Philia

In the Greek there are four main meanings for love. Agape, eros, philia and storge. Agape love is God's love for us. Eros is the love you have for your husband, a romantic love. Storge is empathetic love. And Philia is friendship love. My friend used this term Philia to portray her love for me, as found in the Scriptures.

We went back and forth for the better part of the morning, talking and discussing how bitterness can creep in even if we have said it never would. I then said, "I guess I just need to identify if it is actually bitterness that is creeping in or is it just sadness…"

So I prayed, and I know she prayed right along with me to identify right where I was at.

This is where I found myself, this is where God assured me I was at.

Bitterness vs sadness

I looked up the definition of both, trying to gain a better understanding of each one and their meaning. Am I allowing bitterness to creep in or is it just sadness? What I found was that bitterness has a sharpness, a harshness to it. It includes hatred, resentfulness, cynicism, and hostility. Whereas sadness is sorrow, grief, dejection, melancholy, broken heartedness, and heartache. So, where do I find myself? How do I know for sure that a root of bitterness is not taking hold? I know by the characteristics of bitterness. The sharpness, the harshness, the hatred, and the resentful, cynical, and hostile attributes of bitterness, I do not see or feel within myself. Now sadness on the other hand… I do feel sorrow, grief, broken-heartedness, and heartache. *"Why, my soul, are you downcast? Why so disturbed within me?"* Psalm 42:11 (NIV)

I bring this up because I feel it is a great example of looking inward, discerning a situation, and examining your heart and soul. God's Word is there to help in the discernment process. Pray for insight, and pray for friends to come alongside you and use their gifts of the Spirit to help aid you in your walk.

Pray for the gift of discernment for your husband. And pray for friends to surround him who will use their own discerning gifts to speak into his life.

Prayer

Dear Lord,

     I pray Lord that my husband would be open to challenges brought forth by his friends, and that he would willingly listen and discern what they are saying. Your Word says that wounds from a friend can be trusted. I ask for the gift of insight and discernment both for my husband and myself. I pray that we can both look to Your Word, look inward, and seek what You are telling us. In Your name, Lord God, I pray. Amen.

Notes

My Prayer

Day 6
Wisdom

*"Don't be impressed with your own wisdom.
Instead, fear the Lord and turn away from evil."*
Proverbs 3:7 (NLT)

Solomon, the youngest son of King David, was crowned king when he was just 20 years of age. We find ourselves in 1 Kings chapter 3, where King Solomon is building his palace and the temple of the Lord. In the passage, we see that Solomon showed his love for the Lord by following the instructions given to him by his father, David. After a night of offering thousands of burnt offerings at the altar in Gibeon (the most important high place, and because the temple to the Lord was not yet complete), the Lord appeared to Solomon in a dream and said, *"Ask for whatever you want me to give you"* 1 King 3:5 (NIV)

What a mighty and powerful offer! Imagine your husband being asked this very question; what do you think his response would be?

Without hesitation Solomon responds, *"You have shown great kindness to your servant, my father David, because he was faithful to you and righteous and upright in heart You have continued this great kindness to him and have given him a son to sit on the throne this very day. Now, Lord my God, you have made your servant king in place of my father David. But I am only a little child and do not know how to carry out my duties... So give your servant a discerning heart to govern your people and to distinguish between right and wrong."* 1 Kings 3:6-7,9a (NIV)
Out of everything that King Solomon could have asked for, he asked for a discerning heart so he could govern those under his care.

In response the Lord said, *"Since you have asked for this and not for long life or wealth for yourself, nor have asked for the death of your enemies but for discernment administering justice. I will give you a wise and discerning heart"* 1 Kings 3:11-12a (NIV)

Solomon went on to be the wisest of kings to ever reign because he was watching over God's people. All this because he asked the Lord for a discerning heart. And he was blessed with the gift of wisdom and discernment. James 1:5 (NIV) says *"If any of you lacks wisdom, you should ask God, who gives generously to all without finding fault, and it will be given to you"*

Pray for wisdom and a discerning heart for your husband. Ask God to provide such insight and ability. *"In the same way, wisdom is sweet to your soul. If you find it, you will have a bright future, and your hopes will not be cut short"* Proverbs 24:14 (NLT)

Prayer

Dear Lord

I ask for wisdom for my husband, a discerning heart, and insight into all matters. These are a gift that come from You alone. As we see with Solomon, he didn't want selfish things; he wanted the ability to help discern, and to be the leader he needed to be. He asked for exactly what he needed to lead his people well. In the same way, Lord, I ask for exactly what my husband needs to lead our family well. Help us ask for what we know we need and what we don't know we need. May he lean on You for support, talk with You, and lead his family with You in the middle. Your Word, Lord, says that if we lack wisdom, all we have to do is ask, and You will give it to us generously and without fault. So, I am here coming to You today in Your name and asking for wisdom for both myself and my husband. In Your precious name I pray. Amen.

Notes

My Prayer

Day 7
Marriage

"So they are no longer two, but one flesh. Therefore what God has joined together, let no one separate"
Mathews 19:6 (NIV)

God designed marriage as a covenant between a man and a woman. *"Therefore shall a man leave his father and his mother, and shall cleave unto his wife: and they shall be one flesh."* Genesis 2:24 (KJV)

What exactly does cleave unto his wife mean? Dictionary.com describes it as to adhere closely; stick; cling; to remain faithful.

And they shall be one flesh...

In marriage, you become one flesh by the joining together of two people, a oneness in body, in emotions, in space, and in finances. You are to look to the needs of your husband and he to you. You are to share in the joys and the upsets and to come side by side and serve the Lord together as one.

In Genesis 2, we get a better sense of one flesh. In v. 18 (NIV) we see where God says that, *"It is not good for man to be alone. I will make a helper suitable for him."* So God caused Adam to go into a deep sleep. God took a rib out of Adam and created Eve from Adam's rib. When the man, Adam awoke, he said *"This is now bone of my bones and flesh of my flesh; she shall be called 'woman,' for she was taken out of man."* v.23. In v. 24 the institution of marriage is created. *"That is why a man leaves his father and mother and is united to his wife, and they become one flesh."* Eve was created from Adam's rib, bone of my bones and flesh of my flesh. We see a reference to this in Ephesians 5:28-29 : *"In this same way, husbands ought to love their wives as their own bodies. He who loves his wife loves himself. After all, no one ever hated their own body, but they feed and care for their body, just as Christ does the church—"* What Paul is saying here is a gentle reminder to our husbands we are a part of them. Women were made from the flesh of man. A husband needs to care for his wife just as he would care for himself—in flesh, in bone, spiritually and physically. He needs to honor, cherish, love, and support his wife with everything that he has.

However, our relationship with our Heavenly Father needs to come first. We need to seek time with Him to get to know Him and who we are in God's eyes. Second is your husband. Third are your children. Now this does not mean we ignore our children's needs; it just means we show and demonstrate the importance of the husband and wife relationship to our children. You do this by making time for one another, just as you do Christ. You go on dates, and you create time and space every day to communicate and be with one another. Do this not at the expense of your children, but for their ultimate benefit by having a unified marital connection. Without God in the center of your marriage, life can be hard. So, make sure you are equally yoked. Now this does not ensure a trouble-free life, but it does make things so much easier. When you have struggles, you can go back to where you both reside in the Scriptures.

As the years pass by, you both should be growing. Your tastes will be changing. Your personalities will be maturing. But make sure that as you grow, you grow together as separate people (different likes and dislikes, possibly different hobbies), just not with separate lives. Marriage is about finding a balance with each other. You will have seasons within your marriage, wonderful amazing seasons, seasons of upset, and seasons of great sorrow. It is easy to move through marriage when all is well, and happiness is present. But what do you do when it's not...

There might be a time in your marriage that shakes your entire foundation, a moment that shatters everything you built and worked so hard towards. It can be a place that brings you to your knees in complete and utter despair and confusion. As you look around at the shattered pieces wondering how on earth you will ever be able to put them back together, you pause, you move closer to the cross and the feet of Jesus, and you pray. You cry out with all that you have left and trust that God is right there in the midst of it all. Remember that your joy is not found in circumstances; it is found in your trust in God. This trust is so complete that as you start picking up those shattered pieces, you remember His promises, not just for you but for your husband as well. As you gather the pieces and start putting them together, you will find that some of those pieces are still missing or they shattered into such small particles that they will never be found. So, take the space that no longer has their piece and fill them with God, with who He is and what He has done for you. Here is where He lies; here is where healing begins. He will fill those holes and make you complete once again. We can't do this without Him. He is our comforter, our healer, our counselor, our hope, and so much more.

Marriage takes three—God, husband, wife. Build upon the foundation of faith with God in the center and as the head. Allow God to cover over all areas of your lives. Marriage is hard work. It takes effort. It takes both of you to do your part. It takes love, forgiveness, tenderness, thankfulness, patience, kindness, and above all else, faith. Have faith in the Lord to fulfill His promises for your marriage. Have faith in your husband to fulfill his calling as a husband, father, and leader in your home. Have faith in yourself to come alongside your husband and encourage him to lead your family well.

Prayer

Dear Lord,

I come to You today to ask for a marriage that is filled with love, peace, hope, and forgiveness. I ask that You would help us find the balance in it all. Help us keep the love and that spark alive, to never give up on studying each other, and to continually learn about each other and ourselves. Give us a heart for You and a heart for each other that can withstand the fiery arrows of the evil one. I ask for Your protection, Lord over my marriage, so we can maintain a strong unity with one another. I pray that my husband will leave and cleave and hold fast to me, and that he would step up when and where needed to be the man and husband that he needs to be. We call upon Your name today, Lord God, that You would spread a covering over our marriage. Unite us as one flesh and one body, Lord, so we are able to create a union so special and so unique to who we are. Bless us today Lord, keep us today Lord, and bind us to who You are. In your name Lord, I pray. Amen

Notes

My Prayer

Day 8
Future

*"Many are the plans in a person's heart,
but it is the Lord's purpose that prevails."*
Proverbs 19:21 (NIV)

Imagine, if you will, a nice set of sterling silver. A box full of silverware, a matching tea set with the teakettle, the sugar bowl, and the creamer pitcher. Imagine the beauty that it exudes, and the awe that it can evoke. The shine that can be seen as it sits in the middle of the table being used for the exact purpose that it was intended for.

Now imagine the same sterling silver set, the life that it has had. Maybe during its use, it was dropped a time or two and now has a few dents and dings that occurred along the way. As its purpose in life has come to a stall, it is packaged up, maybe in paper towels or maybe in a special cloth intended to store such fine pieces. As the years go by, it is taken out, dusted off, and looked at a time or two. Years of dirt, grim, and dust have accumulated and stuck to the surface and ingrained itself into the fine lines and intricate designs that its maker so carefully placed with intention.

Now imagine yourself and your Maker, who designed you with intention and care, knowing every hair on your head, and knowing you as you were intricately woven in your mother's womb. You were made on purpose for a purpose. But life... life has taken its toll. Along the way, you have been dropped, dented, and dinged. You have removed yourself from your purpose, and when you look back over your life, you can see the buildup of dirt, grim, and dust that has made its way in, has stuck to your surface, and ingrained itself into your own fine lines and intricate design.

Now imagine those years of buildup. You grab a cloth and cleaner, and you gently start to scrub the sterling silver tea set. You move in circular motions at first, and then up and down, taking the corner of the cloth and getting deep into the lines of the design to remove each layer that has been built up. It takes time. It takes patience. And it takes endurance. It takes the right tools and trust that in the end, the polishing will create something that has been restored to its beauty.

God is working in your life in this same way. He is polishing you and your husband.

He is removing every stain, every speck of dirt, grime, and dust that has settled into His work of art. He has to be careful to use just the right polish for just the right person because what worked for some might be too much or too harsh for others. What worked on me might just take some of your own self away. God knows you intimately, and He knows what it will take, what circumstances are needed, and what polish He has to use to bring you to where you need to be. God is methodical and patient as He cleans you in each and every movement and motion with a purpose. He is cleaning every one of us in the way in which we need. He is preparing us for our future. He is preparing us for what we are to become, His handiwork, to do His will.

The process is not always easy. It can be hard, and it can be painful at times. But know that God is there doing His redemptive work to bring you back to your purpose and shine, to prepare you for what He has in store, and to set you up for your calling. The life that you have lived and the experiences that you have experienced are all so you can grow into who you need to be to fulfill His purposes in your life.

"For I know the plans I have for you," declares the Lord, "plans to prosper you and not to harm you, plans to give you hope and a future."
Jeremiah 29:11 (NIV)

Prayer

Dear Lord,

      Yes, Lord, at times the dust, the grime, and the stains can seep in. I ask that during my husband's redemptive process that You would do a work so fine in him we will once again shine for his purpose and intent. You know the plans You have for us, and I trust in You, the One who holds it all, to show us the way. Shine your light on our path. Help us bring You along into our here and now and into our future because You alone knows what the future holds, and I ask that we will hold ever so tightly to You as we walk into our calling. In Your name, Lord, I pray. Amen.

Notes

My Prayer

Day 9
Wife – Submission

*"Wives, submit yourselves to your own husbands
as you do to the Lord"*
Ephesians 5:22 (NIV)

Submit - but not less than

This word, submit, has caused so much upset and confusion in the world all because people don't quite understand its meaning in the Biblical sense. When some think of submission, they think of forceful, made to do it, less than, and not out of choice or free will. I mean, even the Lexico dictionary defines it; "The action or fact of accepting or yielding to a superior force or to the will or authority of another person" Not wrong, as we are to submit to God and to our husbands, but that is until we get to the example sentence "They were forced into submission." Ah, right there, this is where we get into trouble with this word. Let's take a moment to redefine what submission in a Biblical sense looks like.

For me the most perfect example of submission, and where we should start, is found in Jesus with the Father. *"Jesus gave them this answer: "Very truly I tell you, the Son can do nothing by Himself; He can do only what He sees his Father doing, because whatever the Father does the Son also does."* John 5:19 (NIV) Here we see Jesus submitting to the Father, God. Yet Jesus is equal to the Father, God. *"I and The Father are one"* John 10:30 (NASB) Jesus, although the Father, was willing to allow the Father authority over His life. Jesus demonstrates His submission all throughout the Scriptures. Most significantly, when He died on the cross for our sins.

We are made in God's image, men and women alike. Paul explains it this way in Galatians 3:28, that we are neither male nor female, for we are all one in Christ Jesus, heirs to the promise. Meaning, we are equal in God's eyes. The same, but different. If we believe in and belong to Christ, then we all have the same destination. We do, however, have different and equally important roles and responsibilities that we should take very seriously.

In Ephesians 5:21 (NIV), we are told to *"Submit to one another out of reverence for Christ."* We submit to each other because we are reverent to and love Christ. But what exactly does Reverence mean? Reverence is a deep respect for someone or something. Respect as a verb is to agree to recognize and abide by. This is so multifaceted it's fascinating. Don't you think? As we uncover one layer, another appears. Because we abide in Christ, we have respect for Christ, and out of respect for Christ comes reverence. From all of this flows our submission not only to each other, husbands and wives, but ultimately to Christ Himself.

Our husbands are called to lead; wives we are called to follow. God created wives as a suitable helper for her husband. *"The Lord said, ''It is not good for man to be alone. I will make a suitable helper for him"* Genesis 2:18 (NIV). A suitable helper, one who comes alongside her husband to encourage, to uplift him, to compliment him, to love him, to give him honor, to respect him, and to submit to him. But don't forget that in submitting, our freedoms are not squashed, and our voices are not diminished. It means we get to stand alongside our husbands as partners in life in the roles that God has given each of us.

Husbands are called to lead their wives with a soft hand, gently guiding, gently leading, and not in dominance or fear, but with gentleness, love, care, and concern. Husbands are to love their wives and not live with them in a way that would cause them to be bitter or resentful.

Ephesians 5:22-23 (NIV) *"Wives, submit yourselves to your own husbands as you do to the Lord. For the husband is the head of the wife as Christ is the head of the church, His body, of which He is the Savior."*

Did you catch that "as to the Lord"? We submit to our husbands because we love and are obedient to the Lord. Let's not forget that in our submission to our husbands, we are not less than. We are not to be led in dominance. Our voices should still be heard. We are not inferior in any way. We submit because we are so madly and deeply in love with Jesus.

Just as we recognize God's authority in our lives as we submit to Him, we must also willingly place ourselves under the authority of our husbands. Even if our husband's stumble and fall and are not behaving in a way worthy of their calling does not mean that we no longer have to submit under our husband's care. Again, it's not about dominance or fear—it's about honoring a husband's God given duty to care for his wife and family. Let's not forget that your husband will be held accountable before God for how he cared for you, for how he led his family, and for how he loved his wife as Christ loved the Church. Did he give himself fully to you, his wife?

As we see, there is great responsibility once a man becomes a husband. Husbands are to respect their wives, to love them as if they were his own body. He is to love her as himself (Ephesians 5:28-29). Because the husband is the head of his wife, his role is pivotal, as his example, and ours, is the Lord. He is to love his wife just as Christ loved the church—doing what it takes to support, strengthen, nourish, cherish, guide and most importantly, lead her and cover her with God's Word. We also see how important the husbands role is in 1 Peter 3:7 (NIV), *"Husbands in the same way be considerate as you live with your wives, and treat them with respect as the weaker partner and as heirs with you of the gracious gift of life, so that nothing will hinder your prayers"*

A Godly husband knows the importance of his relationship with his wife. He knows that as the "weaker" partner, he has to shelter her, comfort her, and honor her. How does a husband honor his wife? By loving her as Christ loves the Church and by giving himself up for her. He must set aside selfish behaviors to benefit the marriage covenant. A Godly husband understands that if he doesn't love and care for his wife as Christ loved the Church, then his very own prayers will go unanswered. There are earthly and spiritual consequences when a husband fails to live a godly life.

As 1 Corinthians 13:5 says, love is not self-seeking. Removing selfishness from our lives paves the way for Christ to work in and through us. We must submit ourselves to one another and bind ourselves in love because we know and understand that Biblical submission is so much more than placing yourself under your husband's authority.

Are you willing in a Biblical sense to allow your husband authority in your life just as Jesus allowed God's authority in His life?

Prayer

Dear Lord,

Be a covering over our lives and guide us to Your Word and teach us how we are to accomplish who we are to be to one another and who we are to be to You. Help both myself and my husband to gain better clarity on what it is to be submissive to one another and not the world's view of submission, but the Biblical truth of what submission is to look like. I ask you Lord that you will instill in my husband a love for me as is shown throughout the Scriptures, so he would love me just as You, Lord, loved the church and gave yourself up for her. I pray for a love so strong within my marriage, God, that he will lead by example and be submissive to You, as Jesus is to the Father, as it flows and starts from the top Lord, and that I will learn then by example how to be submissive to my husband. In Your name, Lord, I pray. Amen

Notes

My Prayer

Day 10
Worship

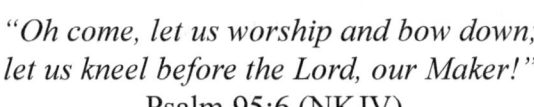

*"Oh come, let us worship and bow down;
let us kneel before the Lord, our Maker!"*
Psalm 95:6 (NKJV)

Have you ever thought about what worship is all about? Have ever wondered how to worship?

Often, we think of worship as a time to sing praises to the Lord, as a time before and after your Pastor gives his sermon, or as a time where we may or may not stand, raise our hands, or sing. We can easily get a false sense of what worship really is. I sometimes hear people who leave service say, "I didn't really get much out of service today." Or they say, "I wasn't too fond of the songs we sang or the message that was given." But we need to stop and realize that worship isn't what we can get out of it. But rather what did God get out of it from you? Why do we worship? We worship because we love and are obedient to the Lord. So, it's really about what I can give, rather than what I can get.

Worship is far more encompassing than just song. It is, and should be, intertwined throughout our entire day in everything that we do from how we raise our family, how we interact with our spouse, and how we show up at work. Are we the same throughout the week as we are on Sunday?

"And whatever you do, whether in word or deed, do it all in the name of the Lord Jesus, giving thanks to God the Father through him."
Colossians 3:17 (NIV)

I remember a time when I was at work listening to worship music and playing with grandbaby up in the mezzanine while trying to get packages ready to ship to customers. Well, baby was getting sleepy, so I paused and gathered her into my arms. Right there, I started worshiping our Heavenly Father as she drifted off to sleep. You see moments like these, moments where we can gather our littles into our arms, cuddle them, snuggle them, and love on them. This is worship to the Lord and sweet worship it is.

Worship is the feeling or expression of reverence and adoration.

How do you express worship? How does your husband express worship? Worship can be the obedience of following the path that God has explicitly set for you. Exercise the skills and talents that you have been gifted with for the purpose of His Kingdom work. Whether you are a stay at home mom, or in the corporate world, and anywhere in between, worship is doing what God built you to do for His glory.

Worship can be different for everyone. In our business, I took the opportunity to pray over every customer as I was packing up products to ship out to them. I was being intentional about what I was doing and allowing the Lord to guide my prayers.

My husband says for him worship is to build. Building things is his inherent gift and skill. He says that building things can be physical in terms of structures and artwork or contrasted in terms of the non-physical and more related to friendships, business partnerships, and relationships. In this, he is able to find worship… in fact, how better is there a way to honor and worship God than to exercise what He has gifted you in the skills, talents, and drive to do?

Not sure what you are built to do? It is easy to find out… Pray and ask. He will tell you. If it is for kingdom work, God will answer you!

In whatever you do, and wherever you go, and whoever you are with, God is in the midst, and He has created us for His glory, not the other way around. What better way to show our love and adoration for the Lord than to enter into His Word daily, to be obedient to His calling, and to do everything in the name of the Lord. All the while, we are giving Him thanks for everything that we have. In fact, it is not the 'doing' of the thing that is worship, rather it is the obedience to follow His leadership in your life and expressing that which He has purposefully and intentionally put inside you. Have you considered what's inside you that has yet to worship Him?

"He is the Maker of heaven and earth, the sea, and everything in them—he remains faithful forever. He upholds the cause of the oppressed and gives food to the hungry. The Lord sets prisoners free, the Lord gives sight to the blind, the Lord lifts up those who are bowed down, the Lord loves the righteous. The Lord watches over the foreigner and sustains the fatherless and the widow, but he frustrates the ways of the wicked. The Lord reigns forever" Psalm 146:6-10 (NIV)

Prayer

Dear Lord,

We ask that you show us what true worship really is and that we would be able to replace what we have thought all this time with truth. I ask that my husband would have an understanding of what true worship looks like and that he would praise You and give You thanks in everything that he does. Help him focus on who You are. To place himself in the middle of worship daily. To focus on You, Lord, in every moment. Help us remember that it's all about You, Lord. In Your name, I pray. Amen

Notes

My Prayer

Day 11
Heart

"A good man brings good things out of the good stored up in his heart, and an evil man brings things out of the evil stored up in his heart. For the mouth speaks what the heart is full of"
Luke 6:45 (NIV)

Our hearts bear the burdens of life. It carries our joys, and our heart breaks. It laughs and cries. It rejoices and mourns. But what does it carry on the regular? What is its natural state? Is it one of tremendous joy or is it tremendous sadness or is it somewhere in between? We carry around our wounds on our hearts. These wounds weigh the heaviest and create the most amount of pain.

I have been wounded, as I'm sure most of you have been as well. But God creates beauty out of the ashes. He takes what others dismiss, and He builds them into beautiful, wonderful, amazing people. Some are wounded but healing, some are wounded but healed. They are no longer dismissed because God calls us to Him. God brings us into His arms and calls us His.

Ephesians 6:10-18 talks about the armor of God.
- Belt of truth
- Breastplate of righteousness
- Shoes for feet, with the readiness that come from the Gospel of peace
- Shield of faith
- Helmet of Salvation
- Sword of truth
- Pray in the Spirit

The armor of God is much like that of a soldier's armor. Each piece is there for a purpose. Each piece helps hold the other up. You see, a soldier's belt wasn't just an accessory piece. In fact, it was a very important piece of the armor, which all other pieces fastened onto. The belt of the soldier was his foundational piece. Just like the truth is the center and foundation of the armor of God.

Once we place the belt of truth around us, we can then start to build the rest of our armor. Next comes the breastplate of righteousness. Righteousness (justice) is given when someone believes, repents, and is filled with the Holy Spirit. Meaning, we are made righteous (just) because Jesus died on the cross for our sins. And through our faith, we are forever made right with God.

Shoes for feet, with the readiness that comes from the Gospel of peace. How on earth can shoes be attached to your belt, you might ask? When the soldier needed to take his shoes off for whatever reason (crossing a waterway perhaps), he attached them to his belt for safekeeping. Not only that, the soldiers shoes had heavy soles that protected his feet and provided traction along the way. As we carry the Word of God in our hearts this gives us the ability to travel the rough roads in life. It helps equip us to maneuver and carry the gospel to others.

Shield of faith: Faith is to be used as our shield when the enemy tries to strike. If our belt of truth, breastplate of righteousness, and our shoes are securely in place, we can confidently hold up our shield of faith. We can confidently, in all circumstances, extinguish the flaming darts of the enemy.

Helmet of Salvation: This is a covering for our head, our mind to help us remember that we have been saved. This is a way to once again combat the enemy when he casts shadows of doubt and discouragement into our minds. This is why meditating (filling our minds) with God's Word is important. So, we can look back quickly to protect and to cover us in times of need.

Sword of truth: This is the Word of God. Knowing the Word and its meaning is of great importance. God left us His Word so we can get to know who He is. So, we can understand better how to move through this life in the joys and sorrows to be ready, combat ready with God's Word. In every situation, be prepared for what is to come, so you can effectively defeat the enemy.

Pray in the Spirit: Pray by yourself. Pray together with your spouse, and together with your friends, family, church, and others. We are called to be in constant prayer. Prayer is our battle cry. Prayer is how we start the battle. Prayer is how we get through the battle. Prayer is how we finish the battle.

How do we move forward with God's armor? We often try to protect ourselves with our own armor. We put on these layers, and we place around ourselves what we think is impenetrable walls. The problem is we cannot protect ourselves. The "armor" that we place on ourselves does not suffice. It is not real. It is not of God. We need to shed the old and put on the new. Take off the armor of your old self and put on the armor of God. All those pieces, all those layers you placed on yourself to "protect" yourself, they start to come off as you place God's armor on. This happens as you trust Him to protect you, and as you trust Him to place the right people in your life to come alongside you to help guide you, to comfort you, and to love you. These all happen one step at a time. Belt of truth, breastplate of righteousness, shoes for feet/put on readiness, gospel of peace, shield of faith, the helmet of salvation, sword of truth, pray in the Spirit. Each one is there for a reason. Each one has its purpose. Each one is equally important as the next.

We place deflective shields onto ourselves, around our thoughts, our minds, and our feelings, but mostly around our hearts to guard our hearts from the pain of the outside world—perhaps even from the pain of letting others in. But forgetting, all the while, the pain of shutting people out. I always said, "Guard your heart" meaning to protect it from going too far and protect it from allowing you a moment of vulnerability. These were all good things, but I gained another perspective. God said to me, "You are to guard your heart with my Word with who I say that you are, and not what the world claims you to be. *"Above all else, guard your heart, for everything you do flows from it."* Proverbs 4:23 (NIV)

Guard your hearts with God's Word and not with our pain, our failures, and our heartbreak—not with walls or barriers or mistrust (as though these would protect us). So, we have to drop those walls, drop the baggage, and allow God's Word to infiltrate our hearts. To take on the armor of God, we need to cover our hurts to prepare us for the things to come.

Pray for your husband's heart to be a heart like David's, one after God's own heart. Pray for your husband to return to or to stay in a heart of worship because out of the overflow of the heart the mouth speaks. We want to freely speak God's words to those around us.

Prayer

Dear Lord,

I ask You Lord that you would mend the brokenness, and that You would heal the wounds we are carrying around in our hearts. I ask for true healing that we would be able to open ourselves up completely to one another and to others. I ask that what is in our hearts is joy, peace, and happiness. I ask that these things would be our overflow. In the midst of deep hurt and pain, it will be the joy, the peace, and the happiness that others see and hear. Not that we are to diminish our pain, but better to say that we use our pain to spur each other on. We use our pain to comfort those around us, and we use our pain to help mend and heal others. Lord, we can't do this on our own, and we need You in the midst of our lives—the good, the bad, and everything in between. In Your name, Lord, I pray. Amen

Notes

My Prayer

Day 12
Mind

"and that you be renewed in the spirit of your mind"
Ephesians 4:23 (NASB)

We are to fill our minds with God's Word and meditate on the Scriptures (filling our minds). Our minds and the minds of our husbands are wide open caverns, waiting to be filled with whatever comes our way. We have to be diligent in our thought life, diligent in a prayer life, and diligent in what we allow in. Taking every thought captive.

In order for us to take our thoughts captive, we need to first renew our minds. We do this by being in the Word daily. 2 Corinthians 10:5 (NIV) says, *"We demolish arguments and every pretension that sets itself up against the knowledge of God, and we take captive every thought to make it obedient to Christ."* We cannot allow our minds to sit idle or to read and view things that will corrupt us. We have to be fully aware and fully awake to the world around us. We are to renew our minds, and to transform our minds. Colossians 3:2 says, *"Set your minds on things above, not on earthly things"* We must be able to use our minds to discern Spiritual truths. 1 Corinthians 2:14 says that We must put aside earthly ways of thinking and take on God's truths in order to follow His ways in our lives. Filling our minds with God's Word is the only way we can be free from the world by trusting in His transforming power over our minds and our lives.

Have you ever thought about what taking our thoughts captive really means? When I think of the word captive, I think of a prisoner being taken away in chains, being led away with purpose and intention—to be in charge of and in command of that person. This is how we are to be about our thought life. We are in charge of our thoughts, and we are in control of what our mind lingers on and for how long. We don't just want to move our thoughts from one place to another, but rather we are to take charge of them, to take them captive and in chains and then lead them away and discard them. Then we are to replace them with something better. If your husband struggles with this, seek God and ask for His touch, His healing, His guidance, and grace to help him take every thought captive.

As Philippians 4:8 (NIV) says *"Finally, brothers and sisters, whatever is true, whatever is noble, whatever is right, whatever is pure, whatever is lovely, whatever is admirable—if anything is excellent or praiseworthy—think about such things."*

Prayer

Dear Lord,

  There is so much in the world that can capture our minds and our thoughts. I ask that You would create a space in the mind of my husband, one that is able to take every thought captive. To remove and replace negative, hurtful thoughts and replace them with thoughts of who You are, thoughts of love, of peace, of happiness and joy. We can't do this on our own, and we might need reminding every once in a while. But with You, Lord, all things are possible. We trust in You today to allow us to take every thought captive. In Your name, Lord, I pray. Amen.

Notes

My Prayer

Day 13
Insecurities

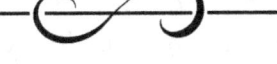

"For nothing will be impossible with God"
Luke 1:37 (NASB)

Insecurities can appear in many forms—in doubt, in fear, in misplaced trust in others, and in worry. Insecurity can also exhibit itself in a lack of confidence in yourself or others.

I remember a Sunday at church when the women gathered at the women's retreat, so we only had just one service that day. In an effort to include the children who are not typically in service, our Pastor came up with a really fun way to include them. Do you remember the game Who Wants to be a Millionaire? He called the "contestants," unbeknownst to them, and then he introduced them. He finally came to the adult team… Well, he called my name, "Aaaaaaaah, what?!" At first, I just sat there not realizing that it was my name, and then I had a wave of feelings come over me. The two that I can remember most were shock and panic. You see, I used to be this super shy girl. When I was younger, I wouldn't even talk to my cousins. When dating my husband, we would play games with his family. I would shrink into him and say, "I will just be on his team," and then I would say absolutely nothing. But I digress. As I was walking to the front of the sanctuary to play the game, I didn't even hear our Pastor's introduction of me because panic had taken over. You know the kind of panic where your cheeks get hot, you start shaking all over, and you only have tunnel vision? Yeah, that kind of panic. Not sure where to go, I head towards my friend, Anthony. He reached out, grabbed my hand and helped me onto the stage. In that moment, my panic started to subside. I gained my internal composure, gave myself a pep talk, and said this is who you were, and not who you are. You are not that shy girl anymore. You got this. You can do this. The panic started to melt away, my shaking started to melt away, and guess what, I survived. I had fun. And I would do it again in a heartbeat!!

Sometimes in life, our old self tries to resurface. It rears its ugly head and says, "Remember that person? Remember who you once were? You are too shy to have fun in front of everyone. You don't know enough to get the answers right. You don't have what it takes to shine your light before others." Please remember that whatever your old self comprised, it does not exist in you today. That is, Who. You. Were. Not who you are! And when you have friends willing to extend to you a helping hand (maybe not even knowing how much in that moment of quiet panic they helped). And in my experience, it was God Himself at work, and sometimes it's just the gentle gesture of an outstretched hand that can mean the world, that can quiet a screaming soul, and that can bring you back to center. They help you remember who you are in Christ; you are someone who is meant to shine their light before others, and someone who, despite fear, conquers the task at hand.

God wants us to rise above our insecurities, to rise above our past, to rise above our fears, and to rise above our doubts. God gives us the strength needed to press forward, and sometimes, he gives us the strength of others to help us through.

Prayer

Dear Lord,

There will be times when insecurity rears its ugly head. I ask for inner strength, Godly friends and an internal narrative of Your Words running through my head to help me and my husband through. That our own insecurities would not be a hindrance to one another or hold us back from pursuing each other or the calling that You have placed on our lives. I ask You Lord for Your hand over our lives, that You would comfort us in times of need and comfort us when insecurities arise. In Your name, Lord, I pray. Amen

Notes

My Prayer

Day 14

Past

"This means that anyone who belongs to Christ has become a new person. The old life is gone; a new life has begun!"
2 Corinthians 5:17 (NLT)

    We all have this tendency to cling to our sadness and allow our hurt and pain to drive us forward. When you are so bound in the brokenness and pain, you forget to look up and see that you need to move forward beyond the pain. We move through life allowing the pain to make our decisions for us. We have to be willing to give those moments of brokenness and hurt to the Lord. We need to learn, and remember, that God has released us from the past. He has released us from the brokenness, and He has released us from the pain. We cannot continue to allow our pain to be our motivators. We bring our past with us into our future and in turn we miss out on what our future really holds. Because we can get stuck, stuck in the past, stuck in the pain, stuck in the sadness, stuck in the present, and stuck in the what ifs. Sometimes the past and the what ifs can consume and overshadow where we are meant to go. We have to release the past, the what ifs, the heartache, and the pain to really move forward, in our healing and in our lives. Allowing God to do a redemptive work in us and through us.

    In the Scriptures, we see many times that when someone is in a season of change God will give them a new name. Saul persecuted many Christians, *"breathing out murderous, threats against the Lords disciples"* Acts 9:1 (NIV), and this went on for several years. But Saul was stopped on the road to Damascus *"suddenly a light from heaven flashed around him."* Acts 9:3 (NIV) Here, Saul had an encounter with Jesus. During this encounter, Saul was made blind. He was led into Damascus, following

Jesus' instructions. There, Saul remained blind for 3 days and did not eat or drink anything. Meanwhile, Jesus was preparing Ananias to meet with Saul.

Upon Ananias meeting with Saul he said, *"Brother Saul, the Lord Jesus, who appeared to you on the road by which you were coming, has sent me so that you may regain your sight and be filled with the Holy Spirit."* Acts 9:17 (NASB). The Scriptures continue with, *"And immediately there fell from his eyes something like scales, and he regained his sight"* Acts 9:18 (NASB). He got up and was baptized. After taking some food, he regained his strength.

Saul spent time with the disciples, the very people he intended to persecute. At once, he began to preach in synagogues that Jesus is the Son of God. What we have to remember is that Saul studied under Gamaliel, so he was already learned in the Jewish Scriptures and was well respected. So, his dramatic change in viewing "the Way" would have garnered a lot of attention.

It took time for people to accept and to trust that Saul was a changed man. Not a man pretending to be changed so he could infiltrate their group and wreak havoc on their lives. Saul had to prove himself, gaining or regaining their trust. Earning someone's trust takes time. It takes getting to know who that person is now. Knowing their past, but willing to look beyond who they were, to who they are, and who they are becoming. *"And that is what some of you were. But you were washed, you were sanctified, you were justified in the name of the Lord Jesus Christ and by the Spirit of our God."* 1 Corinthians 6:11 (NIV)

Did you catch that? That is what some of you were… what you were, stating that there was/is a change. You were washed, sanctified, and justified in the name of the Lord Jesus Christ. Amen and amen to our Father in Heaven who is so quick to forgive, so quick to wash us clean, and so quick to sanctify and justify us. In theology, being justified means: declared or made righteous in the sight of God. Despite our mistakes, our missteps, our sins, or the sins done to us, God makes us righteous in His eyes. He makes us clean, as white as snow, so no blemish or blame remains.

Saul became Paul in Acts 13:9 (NIV), *"Then Saul, who was also called Paul,....."* He became the driving force for the first Christian Churches and the driving force for spreading the Gospel.

Not only was God preparing Saul, He spent time preparing others to help Saul release his past and move forward into his future as Paul. Think about this, God is doing the same for you and me, and He is doing the same for your husband. Each person is placed or allowed in our lives on purpose and for a purpose.

God can and will do a redeeming work in your husband. His promises to us are:

Abundant life:
*"The thief comes only to steal and kill and destroy;
I came that they may have life, and have it abundantly."*
John 10:10 (NASB)

Finish the work He started:
"being confident of this, that he who began a good work in you will carry it on to completion until the day of Christ Jesus."
Philippians 1:6 (NIV)

All things will work out for good:
"And we know that all things work together for good to those who love God, to those who are the called according to His purpose."
Romans 8:28 (NKJV)

God will do a work in your life and in the life of your husband, and in doing so bring things to right. In every one of our circumstances, God is there in the midst. He is preparing us and preparing others to work together to move forward. *"I press on toward the goal to win the prize for which God has called me heavenward in Christ Jesus."* Philippians 3:14 (NIV)

Prayer

Dear Lord,

Our pasts are filled with many hurts, many joys, and many of our own sins as well as the sins of others. I pray that we can lay aside those sins and be washed clean to be justified before You and in Your eyes. Please wipe away all the shame and guilt that one might be feeling. *"Godly sorrow brings repentance that leads to salvation and leaves no regret, but worldly sorrow brings death"* 2 Corinthians 7:10 (NIV). Produce in my husband a Godly sorrow, sorrow that will not bring him to shame, but one that will bring him to You. Use our pasts for Your purpose and plan. Use our lives and what we have gained through our experiences to minister to those around us. To minister to each other. Lord, You are worthy of all of our praise. In Your name, I pray. Amen

Notes

My Prayer

Day 15
Strongholds

*"For the word of God is living and active and sharper than any
two-edged sword, and piercing as far as the division of soul
and spirit, of both joints and marrow, and able to judge
the thoughts and intentions of the heart"*
Hebrews 4:12 (NASB)

In the story of David and Goliath, David has arrived at the battle lines just in time to hear the army shouting the war cry. David begins to ask questions *"What will be done for the man who kills this Philistine and removes this disgrace from Israel? Who is this uncircumcised Philistine that he should defy the armies of the living God"* 1 Samuel 17:26 (NIV)

But David was only met with anger and frustration, and they were quick to dismiss what he had to say. David was steadfast in his mission of facing Goliath that day. His mission was one where he placed the Lord above all else by knowing in his heart of hearts that God was with him and would protect him as He had done before with the lion and the bear. After David gives his "defense," King Saul finally trusts David enough and allows him to press forward and face Goliath.

King Saul dressed David in his very own tunic and coat of armor, but David, not used to such attire, shed the tunic and coat of armor and went out before Goliath as himself. He was not going as what someone else wanted him to be, but with vulnerability, with five stones, and with his sling, David set out. Despite the sheer size of Goliath and the insults being hurled towards him, David remained unfazed. His response to Goliath was *"You come against me with sword and spear and javelin, but I come against you in the name of the Lord Almighty, the God of the armies of*

Israel, whom you have defied. This day the Lord will deliver you into my hands..." 1 Samuel 17:45-45a (NIV)

We see the growth of a shepherd boy not only defeating his giant, but those along the way that had little to no faith in the capabilities that David had until he was able to speak to someone of authority (King Saul) about his own faith and what he felt the Lord placed on his heart. We see Saul taking a chance on a young shepherd boy to come in and make a change that was much needed. It was a change that could bring down the giant that was facing them all that day.

Growth is not easy, and it is not always comfortable and can be painful at times. But growth comes from the hard work, growth comes from digging deep, as iron sharpens iron, so another person sharpens you.

What areas in your life do you need to grow? What areas do you think your husband needs to grow?

What giants are standing in your way of growth? What giants are standing in your husband's way of growth?

How can you slay those giants to make them fall, so you can run victorious into the next season, the next chapter that God has set out before you?

Remember that God is standing with you in that field with only your rock and your sling. Whatever obstacles are in your way today, rest in His promises, and rest in the knowledge that the giant will fall.

Prayer

Dear Lord,

At times, there will be giants that are standing in our way. They will be so big that we might not see past them. I ask for strength and faith such as David had to conquer those giants. With only a sling and five stones, David made his giant fall. But it wasn't without his faith in You,

Lord. Give us such faith and courage to face our giants and to stand in the gap between where we are to where we are going. We cannot do this without You, Lord. As Your Word says *"be strong and courageous! Do not be afraid or discouraged. For the Lord your God is with you wherever you go."* Joshua 1:9 (NLT) You will be with us wherever we go. I hold on to this truth for myself and for my husband. In Your name, Lord, I pray. Amen

Notes

My Prayer

Day 16
Husband

"Husbands, love your wives, just as Christ loved the church and gave Himself up her"
Ephesians 5:25 (NIV)

There is so much responsibility that falls on your husband when you get married. He is now called to be the head of your household. He is now called to lead you and your family both spiritually and sacrificially. He is now called to protect, to love, and to provide. By providing this means to support financially, physically, emotionally, spiritually, and everything else in between. He is now called to love you as Christ loved His church. This is a very large task, and one that is hard work including fearing God and being submissive to God.

Many women don't want to hear this, but women are the weaker sex. This in no way shape or form diminishes who you are. It does not make you less than. By God's design, men and women are made differently. By God's design, He made men physically stronger, capable of caring for, protecting, loving, and providing for his family. Husbands are built by God's design to take on this responsibility. By God's design, He created women to be the nurturers, comforters, and caretakers of the family who are to come alongside their husbands to support and to cultivate the family dynamic.

"Husbands in the same way be considerate as you live with your wives, and treat them with respect as the weaker partner and as heirs with you of the gracious gift of life, so that nothing will hinder your prayers"
1 Peter 3:7 (NIV)

Husbands, if not careful in the way they treat their wives, will have their own prayers hindered. A husband's prayer can be obstructed and or delayed. If your husband is not caring for you as the Lord instructs with grace, mercy, love, and respect, as the weaker partner and as heirs with you, he runs the risk of his prayers being unheard and unanswered.

As I was speaking with my husband on this matter, he said that he feels there is an eternal consequence if a husband misuses, mistreats, or leads his family astray. He says that a husband better be confident, dead confident, in the decision that he is making because a husband must lead his family well. As we see in 1 Peter 3:7, a husband's prayer will be hindered if he doesn't treat his wife with respect. 1 Timothy 5:8 says that if anyone does not take care of his household, he is worse than an unbeliever. 2 Corinthians 5:10 says that when we appear before God on judgement day, we will get what is due us for everything that we have done, good or bad. The Scriptures also tell us we will have to give an account for every careless word that we speak. James 4:17 states that if we know the right thing to do and we don't do it, that is sin. This shows me that your husband will have to stand up and take account of if he has led his family well.

Husbands are commanded to love their wife. *"Husband's, love your wives, just as Christ loved the church and gave Himself up for her"* Ephesians 5:25 (NIV). A husband is to be considerate to his wife and to not be harsh with her, but to treat her with respect. How is he to love his wife? *"In this same way, husbands ought to love their wives as their own bodies. He who loves his wife loves himself. After all, no one ever hated their own body, but they feed and care for their body, just as Christ does the church."* Ephesians 5:28-29 (NIV) He is to follow Christ's example by caring for his wife in the same way that Christ cares for the church with love, compassion, grace, mercy, forgiveness, and understanding. The Scriptures even go as far to say that a husband is to love his wife as his own body. He is to love her as himself. He is to be the same man inside the home as he is outside of the home in front of friends and in the church. God sees, and God knows.

A husband is, *"to make her holy, cleansing her by the washing with water through the word"* Ephesians 5:26 (NIV) This is one of my new favorite verses because it challenges husbands to lead their wives in their spiritual journey with Christ. Charles Spurgeon says, "Christ sanctifies and cleanses us by the washing of water, but what sort of water? By the Word. The water which washes away sin, which cleanses and purifies the soul, is the Word." I would urge your husband to write this verse down, and to memorize this verse, as it sums up perfectly his role in your life. Everything else falls into place when your relationship with the Lord is front and center. Now this does not give you a free pass to not delve into Bible study and quiet time on your own, quite the contrary. This helps open the floodgates of intimacy with the Lord and with your husband. He is to come alongside of you, to encourage, to pray for, to pray with you, and to guide you.

He is to cover you with God's Word.

Prayer

Dear Lord,

There is so much responsibility as a husband. I ask that you would equip my husband to be the man that You have intended him to be. I pray that he can be the husband who he is called to be. May he take his role and responsibilities seriously. I pray that he would respect me and not be harsh with me, and that he would love me, care for me, protect me, and most importantly, cover me in Your Word. I pray that he would be so bold to walk beside me in who You are and bring us both up to the level in which you desire. I also ask that I would come alongside my husband to invest in him, to spend time with him, to encourage him, and to recognize his place in our relationship. May I meet his needs as he meets mine. In Your precious name, I pray. Amen

Notes

My Prayer

Day 17
Wife – Equal

―――――――∽○――――――――

"So God created mankind in His own image, in the image of God He created them, male and female He created them"
Genesis 1:27 (NIV)

Equal - but different

You and your husband were created in the image of God. You were created equal, but different. You were made on purpose for different purposes.

Genesis 1:27-28 (NIV), *"So God created mankind in His own image, in the image of God He created them; male and female He created them. God blessed them and said to them, "Be fruitful and increase in number; fill the earth and subdue it. Rule over the fish in the sea and the birds in the sky and over every living creature that moves on the ground."* Men and women were both created in the image of God, male and female. Together they have a command set before them, and a blessing from the Lord to be fruitful and to rule over the earth — side by side as husband and wife, Genesis 1:29-30 (NIV), *"God saw all that he had made, and it was very good. And there was evening, and there was morning—the sixth day."* Genesis 1:31 (NIV) God was pleased with His creation, not only with Adam and Eve, but with the day and the night, with the animals, with the sky, with the water, with the ground, and with the plants — all working together. In Genesis 3:16-19, we see a shift. We are still equal partners, we just have different roles. This shift happens because of the fall, and the discipline that God handed down to Adam and Eve. From this stems the age old argument of whose fault it was. Eve's because she knew they were not to eat of the fruit and presented it to her husband (Genesis 3:2)? Or

Adam's because he did not stop his wife from taking the fruit off of the tree and taking a bite (Genesis 3:6)? Or both with equal responsibility to the fall of mankind? Both knew better, but neither one of them did anything to stop it from occurring. Just as we as parents discipline our children, so does God discipline us. As a result, both Adam and Eve were given their punishment. For Eve, God said, *"I will make your pains in childbearing very severe; with painful labor you will give birth to children. Your desire will be for your husband, and he will rule over you"* (v.16). This is the first time where we see God specifically place the husband as leader of the home and where God says that wives are to submit to the authority of her husband. Because of the fall, Adam's job, man's job, became harder. *"To Adam he said, "Because you listened to your wife and ate fruit from the tree about which I commanded you, 'You must not eat from it,'" Cursed is the ground because of you; through painful toil you will eat food from it all the days of your life. It will produce thorns and thistles for you, and you will eat the plants of the field. By the sweat of your brow you will eat your food until you return to the ground, since from it you were taken; for dust you are and to dust you will return"* (v.17-19).

    Your husband was created to work the land/job, to work with his body/mind, to have endurance, and to protect. You were created to work just as hard, and to have endurance, but you were also given the innate ability to nurture and to care for those around you. Along with these differences, we have physical differences as well. Now understand, this is not an exhaustive list as men and women have many different attributes and God-given roles and responsibilities.

    As wives, we willingly allow our husbands to lead us, to guide us, and to care for us. This means that your husband, as he takes on this leadership role in your marriage, does so with great intention and care just as Jesus willingly allowed the Father to lead, guide, and care for Him.

    We even see Jesus valuing women just as much as men. Jesus welcomed women into His ministry. He openly spoke to and taught women, which went against the culture of the time. Jesus allowed women to support His ministry financially. In a time where women were viewed as "property", viewed as less than, Jesus took that mentality and showed the men something different. He showed them the value of women, and the importance of working with one another. Jesus taught them the importance of the work and effort that women have.

You need to work together as husband and wife to fulfill your God given purpose, and the purpose that God created in advance for you to do. You both need to remember that you have equal importance in God's eyes. You have a job to do. Different yes, but just as hard, just as fulfilling, and just as equal.

Prayer

Dear Lord,

I know Lord that my husband and I were created in Your image, equal but different, and made for different purposes. I ask You Lord that you would help us accentuate our differences, as he was made to protect, and I to nurture, among many things. Guide us in working together to further Your kingdom work. Together may we work towards the same goal. May we be equal, but different. In Your name, I pray. Amen

Notes

My Prayer

Day 18
Prayer

"Do not be anxious about anything, but in every situation, by prayer and petition, with thanksgiving, present your requests to God"
Philippians 4:6 (NIV)

When things seem so far from fair and so far from what we had planned or wished for and when everything is so up in the air that you can barely breathe, God is there in the middle of it all. He is reaching down into the middle of your story. Trust in Him, His promises, and His truths. Right there in the middle of your story, you will find Him there, reaching out to you, gathering you into His loving arms, and saying "I have got this child".

In those times, when you find yourself on your knees in a crumpled mess crying out to the Lord, "Please take this from us, please find favor in our situation, please Lord you are mightier than any law, any person, any situation, and you see the bigger picture here, not my will Lord but Yours be done". Recently, I found myself in this place, crying out to the Lord, literally weeping on my knees, praying as I felt very little control over what was occurring.

While there were many things I found in that moment, what I found most was God's comfort, His peace, His patience with me, His Love for me, His amazing grace, and His mercy. But I also gained a better understanding of what Jesus went through as He prayed on the Mount of Olives in Gethsemane. In the account of Luke, it says that Jesus prayed so hard that His sweat was like drops of blood. He was in anguish over His situation. So, what was His response in this moment? It was to pray more earnestly. We also see that Jesus brought along His friends, and in this moment when they were able to steal away from the rest of the group, He was able to be open and raw with them *"My soul is exceedingly sorrowful, even to death"* Matthew 26:38 (NKJV) He confides. We learn that even Jesus, yes Jesus, needed His friends close to Him during one of His most difficult moments. So, in those moments such as these, when all seems unbearable and unbelievable and your soul is sorrowful, we surround ourselves with our close friends, and they surround us in love, support, and prayers.

God showed us His favor. He showed us His divine power over a situation. He showed us the love of friends who surrounded us and entered into our story to help us, to cry with us, to encourage us, and to fast and pray right along with us.

Let's not forget today that in the midst of our trials, our struggles, and our story, we need to praise Him for what He has already done. We need to praise Him for what He is about to do. I urge you to be so bold and intentional with your relationship with God, not only in your trials but also in your times of rejoicing because we serve a mighty God!!

Prayer

Dear Lord,

Prayer is a powerful thing. It brings us ever closer to You. This is a time and place for us to communicate with You on a personal level to find ourselves at the foot of the cross and bare our souls, so we can learn better who You are and who we are. I pray that my husband has a fruitful and consistent prayer life. May he find the utmost importance in daily time with You. May he cherish every moment he has with You. May he bring me along on his journey in his relationship with You. I pray Lord that my husband would lead me to the cross and pray with me, and that he would lead our family in prayer, in times of struggle, in times of rejoicing, and in times where life is neither of those things. Our relationship with You starts here, with prayer. Help him see the importance of prayer and time spent with You. In Your name, I pray. Amen

Notes

My Prayer

Day 19

Fruit

"that you may walk worthy of the Lord, fully pleasing Him, being fruitful in every good work and increasing in the knowledge of God;"
Colossians 1:10 (NKJV)

As I was reading the story of Jesus and the fig tree in Mark 11:12-14, I realized that I didn't completely understand why Jesus would curse the fig tree. The tree was in leaf, yet Jesus was not happy with what He found. I can imagine the confusion that the disciples may have felt, as I felt that same confusion until I learned that a fig tree grows its leaves just before it bears its fruit. So, when Jesus saw the fig tree from far off, with its leaves in full bloom, He fully expected to see the fig tree bearing its fruit. Jesus fully expected the fig tree to be fulfilling its purpose due to what it was displaying. As Jesus came near to the fig tree, He found that it was not bearing any fruit. It was not fulfilling what it portrayed itself as being. So, He cursed the fig tree and said, *"May you never bear fruit again"* Matthew 21:19 (NIV) The next day as they passed by, they saw that the tree withered just as Jesus had spoken.

This brings me to the following questions. What do people see in you from far off?

What do they see in you when they get close? Are you bearing any fruit underneath your leaves? Or do you only appear to be bearing fruit? If Jesus saw you from far away, would He see the same thing once He got close enough? Now ask these same questions about your husband. Is he the same at home as he is at church? Is he the same with you as he is with his friends and coworkers?

To produce fruit, we must identify where we need pruning. Are you or your husband bearing any fruit? Are we supposed to cut off that which is not producing so that which is producing can grow? Yes, as John 15:2-4 (NIV) explains, *"He cuts off every branch in me that bears no fruit, while every branch that does bear fruit He prunes so that it will be even more fruitful. You are already clean because of the word I have spoken to you. Remain in me, as I also remain in you. No branch can bear fruit by itself; it must remain in the vine. Neither can you bear fruit unless you remain in me."*

Are you and your husband willing to cut off that which isn't producing fruit? Are you and your husband willing to let go of that which is not producing fruit?

If the answer is no, then we must identify why and what needs to be pruned. If we are holding onto something for earthly reasons, then it's no longer about God. If our hand is so tightly clenched that there is no room for anything else to be put in its place, there is no room for growth. There is no room for blessings to flow.

The pruning process is tough, it can be hard, and it can hurt. Imagine taking a sharp pair of pruning clippers and cutting off that which is dead or dying to allow the remaining greenery or flowers to grow. To not allow the dead weight to burden the living and suck the life out of what remains. We all have to go through a similar process to become who God wants and desires us to be. This, in part, is why we are to hide His Word in our hearts, so when the pruning process comes, we are able to understand, identify, and accept what we are going through. And there might be times when we won't understand what we are going through, but this gives us the opportunity to press into our Heavenly Father and trust that He has us in His arms and is guiding us through whatever it is we are going through. We have the knowledge in His word to pull from. To share with others your own process of pruning when theirs is still in its infancy and needs more cultivating and watering to grow.

"I am the vine; you are the branches. If you remain in me and I in you, you will bear much fruit; apart from me you can do nothing. If you do not remain in Me, you are like a branch that is thrown away and withers; such

branches are picked up, thrown into the fire and burned"
John 15:5-6 (NIV)

Pray for Godly fruit in your husband. Pray that he will abide in Christ forever.

Pray that his first thought in the morning is Christ and his last thought before bed is Christ. If he is so consumed in Christ and in your marriage, you will get caught up in the overflow and together you can hold each other accountable to be bearing good fruit.

Prayer

Dear Lord,

Oh Lord, I come to you today and ask that You would help my husband and I identify where we are in need of pruning. Outside of You we can do nothing, but with You and remaining in You Lord, we can bear much fruit. I want the lives of my husband, myself, and my family to be full. May we produce fruit, and not just any fruit, but fruit that is pure and so full of You that people will be able to see it from far off. I ask that You would help us be people who are the same on Sunday as we are during the week. Oh Lord, Your fruit is what I want others to see. In Your name, Lord, I pray. Amen.

Notes

My Prayer

Day 20
Friendship

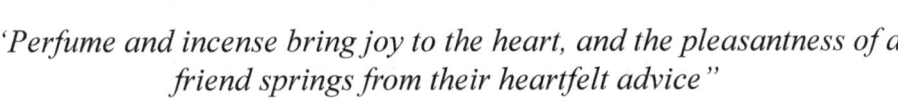

"Perfume and incense bring joy to the heart, and the pleasantness of a friend springs from their heartfelt advice"
Proverbs 27:9 (NIV)

The story of the paraplegic man is a devastatingly overlooked story in the Bible. I say devastatingly because we tend to only focus on the paraplegic man and his physical healing. What we miss out on is the power of faith, the power of friends, the power of forgiveness, and the power of healing.

We know little about the paraplegic man. Was he born this way? Was he injured? What we do know is that he had some very faithful and faith filled friends.

The story begins with people finding out that Jesus was at a home. They gathered in the home, standing room only with no room left, not even outside the door. In the midst of the crowd, we see four men emerge, carrying a paraplegic man. Because of so many people that were in attendance hearing Jesus preach, the men could not reach Him. With determination on their side, they carried the man up the stairs (which were on the outside of the home) onto the roof of the home. They dug a hole in the roof and lowered the man through. They placed him right at the feet of Jesus, smack dab in front of him. Now, imagine if you will, the sheer strength needed to lower a full-grown man incapable of bearing any of his own weight, down through a roof right to the place he needed to be. Now listen closely to what comes next because it is so easily missed. *"When Jesus saw their faith, He said to the paralyzed man, "Son, your sins are forgiven"* Mark 2:5 (NIV). Not only did Jesus forgive the paraplegic man of his sins, He also healed him physically. *"I tell you, get up, take your mat and go home" He got up, took his mat and walked out in full view of them all"* Mark 2:11-12a (NIV).

"When Jesus saw their faith." This is where I want to pause and place our focus on the faith of the paraplegic man's friends. He was healed not only physically but emotionally and eternally because of the faith his friends had. And if you notice, his friends did not ask for anything in return. They did not ask for or require anything for themselves from Jesus. They were so determined and willing to do whatever it took for their friend to see Jesus and for their friend to be healed. They knew in their heart of hearts who Jesus was and what Jesus could do. They acted not out of selfish ambition, seeking nothing in return. They carried their friend, how far we don't know, and held him as they assessed the situation. Realizing that there was no easy way in, they carried him up a flight of stairs, dug a hole, and built a contraption to lower him through the hole all to be placed at the feet of Jesus.

His friends had no other thought in mind except that their friend would be healed and be able to walk himself out of that home. To walk with his friends in fellowship home. To now have the ability to earn a living, get married, and have a family. Because of his friend's faith, it changed the entire trajectory of his life. And Jesus saw, and He knew their heart's desire. In turn, Jesus healed the paraplegic man because of the faith of the man's friends.

They were there to lift and carry their friend when he could not do it on his own. They had the faith to intervene in their friend's life. The power of friendship, the power of faith, and the power of love are all wrapped up in a story so easily missed. Faith on loan.

So I ask you...

Who is in your tribe? Who is in your inner circle? Who is your person? Who can you be raw and vulnerable with? Who can you laugh with, to the point of your sides hurting and tears streaming down your face? Who will be there for you in good times and bad? Who will fast and pray right along with you when the moment calls for it? Who will hold you accountable and gently call you out when needed? Who will stand in their kitchen holding you as you cry and pray over you? Who do you feel safe with? Who do you allow your walls to come crashing down in front of?

I never understood the importance of having all of these things within friendship, or the need of friendship outside of my husband. But when God opened the door, I walked through it in obedience. He showed me. He showed me that doing life with others is so imperative. He showed me what equally yoked friendships look like. He showed me I have to be willing; I have to be open, and I have to be vulnerable and raw.

We see Jesus on several different occasions steal away with His inner circle. We see Him become raw and transparent. We see Him confide in them how He is doing. We see Him doing life with them.

There is no "magic" formula. It's about intentionality because otherwise, it just won't happen. It's about doing things on purpose for a purpose. You have to cultivate it because it just won't grow. You have to pray for it because it just won't prosper on its own.

So, if you know who these people are, pursue them. Be intentional with them. Be vulnerable with them. Pray with them. Pray for them. God will bless your friendships. God will guide your friendships. So please treasure it, value it, protect it, and pray for it.

So, when you and your husband are seeking friendship, search for equally yoked people. Not the same, but those with the same faith. Search and cultivate friendships with others who are like-minded, love Jesus, and those who walk out their faith. Search for friends who will do life with you, not just in the good times, but in the nitty gritty bad times as well. Search for friends who will carry you, and those who will dig a hole in a roof for you and place you at the feet of Jesus.

Prayer

Dear Lord,

     After reading through the story of the paraplegic man's healing and the faithfulness of his friends, I ask that you would bless my husband and myself with friends such as these. Bless me with friends who will carry me when I can't seem to carry myself. May we have friends like Aaron and Hur, who held Moses arms up when he didn't have the strength. I pray that you would place in our lives friends who are more than willing to put their faith on loan when ours seem weak. I pray to have friends who will encourage us, uplift us, call us out when needed, and share life with us. I pray that we would be blessed with Godly, equally yoked friends that we can share our burdens and our joys with. I praise you Lord in Your name, I pray. Amen

Notes

My Prayer

Day 21
Strength/Courage

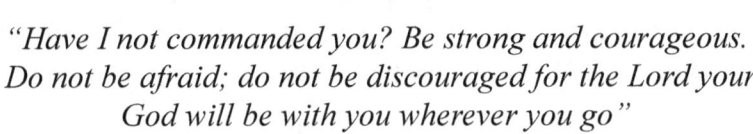

*"Have I not commanded you? Be strong and courageous.
Do not be afraid; do not be discouraged for the Lord your
God will be with you wherever you go"*
Joshua 1:9 (NIV)

In the book of Esther, we read about a young woman who shows just how much strength and courage she has. We see what this can look like, and we see how to garner the inner strength which God provides. As many of you know Esther was a young girl, pulled into a life of preparation. Preparation to go before the king, to see if she or any other girl would find favor in the king's eyes, the one who would then become Queen.

Esther not only found favor in the king's eyes, but she also found favor in the eyes of those who cared for her. Esther was full of courage and strength, a Godly young lady with a teachable spirit, and a young lady who was obedient to the call on her life. She proved herself over and over again in this regard. And this young lady soon became Queen.

Where Esther's strength and courage really shines is when Mordecai approaches her and implores her to go before the king with information about the decree to kill the Jews. But Esther refuses because she knows that she has to be summoned into the king's inner courts. She knows that if anyone goes into the inner courts uninvited, it is certain death. In an effort to get Esther to understand the importance of the situation at hand, Mordecai responds to her refusal with this *"For if you remain completely silent at this time, relief and deliverance will arise for the Jews from another place, but you and your father's house will perish. Yet who knows whether you have come to the kingdom for such a time as this?"* Esther 4:14 (NKJV)

What is Mordecai saying here? He is saying that if you don't do this, if you don't say what needs to be said then God will use someone else.... Whoa, wait a minute, let's take a step back. Mordecai believes with all his heart that Esther was put there at just this time for just this purpose. Have you ever had someone be so confident in what you needed to do that they just kept insisting until you did it? Having an understanding far beyond your own grasp, but you still wanted nothing to do with it? Why? Because it scared you, the odds were stacked against you?

But do I, do you, really want to give up what God has called you to do? So, what do we do in times like these? We test against the Scriptures; we pray with intention, and we pray the Scriptures. I mean, even Jesus Himself prayed the Scriptures, so why shouldn't we? We ask for help and discernment, and once we get confirmation; we pursue.

It doesn't take long for Esther to gain her strength and her courage. She responds to Mordecai with, *"If I perish, I perish"* We see her call in the troops *"go and hold a fast on my behalf, I and my young women will do the same"* Esther 4:16

She spent the next 3 days fasting, and more than likely praying within her fast. Now the Scriptures do not specify if prayer was involved, but many believe that it did. What does it mean to pray and fast? This is an undivided and intense devotion to the Lord, a need and dependence on Him. You can find prayer and fasting in the old and new Testaments in times of mourning, repentance, and deep spiritual need. Now, we are not commanded to fast, but it can be beneficial. Fasting is not just about giving up food, but it can be anything given up temporarily in order to focus all of our attention on God. In the New Testament, we see the Church of Antioch pray and fast and place hands on the 2 men (Saul & Barnabas) before they sent them off to do the Lord's work. Esther gathered her friends around her to join her in her time of fasting. This is yet another example of having Godly friends surrounding you. Esther, despite her fears, moved forward, and despite her fears, she pressed on.

In chapters 5-10, we see the events unfold. Esther gathers the strength and courage to go before the king to shed light on Haman's evil plans. We see her rise to the occasion and press forward in victory and doing something that God has asked or even required of her. Esther, although scared and fearful, pressed forward with God on her side. Not knowing the outcome, but knowing who held the outcome. Knowing that if things didn't go the way it was planned, she knew in the depths of her being that God was the greater factor here and that she would be all right regardless of the king's response.

Prayer

Dear Lord,

I ask You Lord that the same strength and courage Esther had will show up within my husband, within myself. That despite all else, he can maintain an attitude of courage. An attitude of strength. Regardless of what lies ahead, he will press forward, with You by his side. That he would care for his family, maintain his job, his friendships, all with an inner strength that can only come from You. And in order to achieve this Lord, I ask that you give him a heart to be in Your word daily, as this is where we gain our strength and our courage. That You would tug on his heart and he would respond to the call on his life. In the big things, Lord, and in the small. The strength and the courage to fight off temptations, whatever those may look like. The strength and courage to be the man, husband and father that You have called him to be. Oh Lord, as Your word says *"I can do all things through Him who strengthens me"* Philippians 4:13 (NASB) In your precious name Lord I pray. Amen.

Notes

My Prayer

Day 22
Kindness

"Therefore as God's chosen people, holy and dearly loved, clothe yourselves with compassion, kindness, humility, gentleness and patience "
Colossians 3:12 (NIV)

Throughout the Scriptures are many examples and plenty of verses about being kind. I poured over them, trying to find the perfect example of what being kind is all about. I landed here on the good Samaritan.

We see in Luke 10:29-37 (NIV) the good Samaritan. We see a man robbed, beaten, and left for dead on the side of the road. We witness two men, one a priest and one a Levite, crossing to the other side of the road, intentionally going out of their way as to not be bothered with this man. As a Samaritan man was passing by, the Scriptures say *"he took pity on him"*.

He cleaned him up, bandaged his wounds, gathered him onto his donkey, and proceeded to take this injured and dying man to an inn, and cared for him for the night. He instructed the innkeeper to look after the man, paid for the room and for his care, and said *"when I return, I will reimburse you for any extra expenses you may have."* We see a complete stranger take care of this man. So how much more should we take care of our own? To show unending kindness, without the expectation of something in return.

What is kindness? The Lexico dictionary defines it "The quality of being friendly, generous, and considerate"

Okay, but to me this is still a very generalized definition. What are some of the characteristics of kindness?

Your words: we need to speak lovingly, gently, and carefully to our spouse.

> *"Death and life are in the power of the tongue,"*
> Proverbs 18:21a (NASB)

> *" Do not let any unwholesome talk come out of your mouths, but only what is helpful for building others up according to their needs, that it may benefit those who listen."*
> Ephesians 4:29 (NIV)

Your actions: We all remember the old saying that actions speak louder than words. As much as this is true, our actions also need to align up with our words. An example of an action is to do something for your spouse without being asked, without grumbling, and with joy in your heart.

> *"Therefore encourage one another and build up one another, just as you also are doing"*
> 1 Thessalonians 5:11 (NASB)

Your attitude: Do you or your spouse have a calm and gentle spirit? Or are they always grumbling and arguing about time spent, about things that need to be done, etc.?

> *"Let each of you look not only for his own interests, but also for the interests of others"*
> Philippians 2:4 (NKJV)

Your forgiveness: Be quick to forgive. Keep no records of wrongs.

> *"Be kind to one another, tenderhearted, forgiving each other, just as God in Christ also has forgiven you."*
> Ephesians 4:32 (NASB)

> *"It does not dishonor others, it is not self-seeking,*

> *it is not easily angered, it keeps no record of wrongs."*
> 1 Corinthians 13:5 (NIV)

Your empathy/understanding: Are you sensitive to one another in all situations? Are you aware of how the other feels?

> *"Whoever is slow to anger has great understanding,*
> *but he who is quick tempered exalts folly"*
> Proverbs 14:29 (NASB)

Your support: Do you come alongside your husband, and he you, to support each other's dreams and calling? Are you and your spouse there to support and encourage each other when you are down, or excited for what is on the horizon?

> *"Bear one another's burdens, and so fulfill the law of Christ"*
> Galatians 6:2 (NKJV)

> *"Two are better than one, because they have a good return*
> *for their labor: If either of them falls down,*
> *one can help the other up"*
> Ecclesiastes 4:9-10 (NIV)

I would like to sum up with 1 Corinthians 13:4-7 (NIV) where we have a genuine love and lack of selfishness, kindness is sure to follow.

"Love is patient, love is kind. It does not envy, it does not boast, it is not proud. It does not dishonor others, it is not self-seeking, it is not easily angered, it keeps no record of wrongs. Love does not delight in evil but rejoices with the truth. It always protects, always trusts, always hopes, always perseveres."

Prayer

Dear Lord,

 Words are so very important in life and can create a healthy or unhealthy environment. I pray that my husband will be kind in all that he does, in all that he says and in all that he is, including Lord, where firmness is required. If we want to be more like You, Lord, we have to show kindness within our firmness. Your word says that love is patient, and that love is kind. I ask for these to show up in my husband more often than not. That these characteristics and attributes would be his go to. And Lord, if my husband struggles with anger, or has a temper, I ask that you would tug on his heart and that he would be able to feel You in his life and change his heart posture. *"Gracious words are a honeycomb, sweet to the soul and healing to the bones."* Proverbs 16:24. In Your name, Lord, I pray. Amen.

Notes

My Prayer

Day 23
Forgiveness

*"Bear with each other and forgive one another if any
of you has a grievance against someone forgive
as the Lord forgave you"*
Colossians 3:13 (NIV)

Forgiveness does not absolve anyone of their sins. Forgiveness is more for you than anyone else. It is a way for you to move forward. This by no means suggests that you don't take from the situation and learn from it. I think it is one of the first steps for your heart to mend and heal, so you can move forward in your relationship, however that occurs for you. Some feel that if I forgive, then that is saying what that person did was acceptable, and they were "let off the hook" for their sins. This is far from the truth. They still need to confess, repent, restore, and move forward proving themselves trustworthy again. And if restoration can't be had, please know that this does not mean that forgiveness has not been given. There might be times when being in a relationship with the other person is not healthy and not where God has called you to be. You will know this by praying and speaking with God. He will let you know how to proceed and when. Trust in Him to lead you and to guide you throughout this entire process.

So how do we move through forgiveness? How do I pray that my husband has a forgiving heart? We start within the Scriptures.

"Bear with each other and forgive one another if any of you has a grievance against someone. Forgive as the Lord forgave you. And over all these virtues put on love which binds them all together in perfect unity."
Colossians 3:13-14 (NIV)

Love keeps no record of wrongs!!

I thought I was doing this right. I thought just because I was not using my husband's past sins as ammunition when having a disagreement or in any other manner that I had a grasp on what this meant. Now don't read what I am not writing. When something arises, and sin enters the picture, you must discuss and work through it. It's a process, one that you need to bring up whatever sins have occurred and work through them. I am talking about later, much later when you have moved forward from the sin and when you have had a chance to heal and to mend the broken pieces of your shattered moments. Even still, there will be times when discussion will occur, and you move forward once again from there.

God helped me to see that when we make mistakes, and we sin against each other and against Him He does not remember. *"For I will forgive their wickedness and will remember their sins no more"* Hebrews 8:12 (NIV).

So what does this mean? Are we to forget the sins of those who hurt us? I don't think so. Because if we "forget", we are more than likely to place ourselves right back into the same situation. Now, we should not focus on where we have been, rather on where we are going. If we are striving to be more like our Heavenly Father, then we should try to actively not remember. Let me explain. We are not to forget the lessons learned from our sins or the sins of others, but to choose to "not remember" the sin itself. Now, we are not commanded to forget, or not remember, but we are commanded to keep no records of wrongs... Perhaps it's not so much as forgetting, but more about not keeping a list, and not keeping a mental note of what they did wrong. But to allow for errors to occur and forgiveness to enter. To allow for the pain to subside and the process of healing to begin.

The pain can be with you daily, but it's not good for you or for him. We need to keep no records of wrongs. It is our choice what we think about and what we allow to linger in our minds. *"and we take captive every thought to make it obedient to Christ"* 2 Corinthians 10:5b (NIV)

When we stray and sin, repent and return, God says, "Welcome home now let's try this again." To welcome Him in, to welcome your husband in, and remove whatever stain is upon your heart and in your head in order to fully submerge yourself into the faithful arms of God and keep no records of wrong.

Forgiving someone is sometimes a daily decision. If you find yourself in that moment of unforgiveness, talk with God and say, "Lord I have already forgiven my husband, but please help me continue on my path of forgiveness." The Lord will surely help.

"If your brother or sister sins against you rebuke them; and if they repent, forgive them. Even if they sin against you seven times in a day and seven times come back to you saying "I repent", you must forgive them"
Luke 17:3-4 (NIV)

God has extended grace, love, mercy, and forgiveness towards you so choose to do the same towards your husband. Yes, it is a choice you have to make. But remember that forgiving others is a command. If you are struggling in your forgiveness, pray about it with an open and authentic heart. Have nothing but love and forgiveness in your heart, but remember by doing this, it does not excuse or even disregard what they have done. It just gives you the freedom to let go and to know that God has it all under His control. What was intended for harm, God will use for your good.

The best definition of mercy I have heard is this… To release someone from the punishment that they rightfully deserve.

"Above all love each other deeply, because love covers over a multitude of sins" 1 Peter 4:8 (NIV)

Now what about your husband? We need to pray that he will have a heart of forgiveness not only for you but for himself as well.

Whatever he might need forgiveness for, big or small, you need to be there to help encourage, comfort and possibly guide him back to center. And by center, I mean back into the folds of who God is.

"My brothers and sisters, if one of you should wander from the truth and someone should bring that person back, remember this: whoever turns a sinner from the error of their way will save them from death and cover a multitude of sins" James 5:19-20 (NIV)

Or bring them for the first time into the folds of who God is. *"Wives, in the same way submit yourselves to your own husbands so that, if any of them do not believe the word, they may be won over without words by the behavior of their wives"* 1 Peter 3:1-2 (NIV)

Your husband's sin might be causing him great sorrow and grief. And perhaps not. We will get to that in a moment. The Scriptures say, *"Now instead, you ought to forgive and comfort him, so that he will not be overwhelmed by excessive sorrow. I urge you, therefore, to reaffirm your love for him."* 2 Corinthians 2:7-8 (NIV)

Reaffirm your love for him. Try to recall the reasons you fell in love with him, and the reasons you married him. Even in our deepest heartache and pain, we need to be comforters for our husbands. We need to forgive, support, and help them back to who God says that they are. We need to pray that their sin will not overshadow them and cause them excessive sorrow. We need to help reaffirm not only our love for him, but God's love for him because in the midst of coming out the other side of sin, your husband may be grieved greatly and needs to be gently reminded of these things.

Now, if your husband is unrepentant and does not have a heart of sorrow or grief, we need to intercede on their behalf. *"But because of your stubbornness and your unrepentant heart, you are storing up wrath against yourself from the day of God's wrath, when His righteous judgment will be revealed"* Romans 2:5 (NIV). You do not want your husband to get caught up in God's wrath. You need to find yourself at the foot of the cross praying that God will reach into your husband's heart and grab hold, so that your husband will feel that tug on his heart and repent and turn from his harshness and sin. *"Godly sorrow brings repentance that leads to salvation and leaves no regret, but worldly sorrow brings death."* 2 Corinthians 7:10 (NIV)

Forgiveness is not always easy. But it is always fruitful. It will create in you a calm and a peace that you otherwise wouldn't have. We serve a mighty God. Ask, seek, knock. If you ask with the right heart, you seek with the right mind, and you knock for the right reasons, you will receive. You will find, and the door will be opened to you.

"Ask and it will be given to you; seek and you will find; knock and the door will be opened to you. For everyone who asks receives; the one who seeks finds; and to the one who knocks, the door will be opened." Matthew 7:7-8 (NIV)

Prayer

Dear Lord,

I know that it is not always easy and we can't do this on our own. Lord, be with this family, this husband and wife who are in the midst of forgiveness. Bless them, take their pain and sorrow far from them. Help them find healing and rediscovery of one another. Help them know that You are in the midst of all of this and that You can take their situation and use it for good. Show them that forgiveness is there, and as You forgive so must we forgive. You are our guide and example of how we are to be; You have shown us grace and mercy and now it's time for us to show grace and mercy. Thank you, Lord for being faithful and true. That in the midst of pain and struggle we can all still find joy, because joy is found in You. We praise You Lord and love You Lord! In Your name, we pray. Amen.

Notes

My Prayer

Day 24
Intimacy

"His left arm is under my head, and His right arm embraces me"
Song of Songs 2:6 (NIV)

What does authentic intimacy look like? Intimacy is composed of a touch, a look, encouraging words, time spent, honesty, compassion, forgiveness, service, and so much more. It is being close to one another, and yes, intimacy also includes sex.

In fact, the definition of intimacy is: close familiarity or friendship; closeness. A private, cozy atmosphere. An intimate act, especially sexual intercourse.

Intimacy is not about expecting something in return from the other. Intimacy is about being there for each other, filling their emotional needs first. Often, when we think of intimacy, our minds go directly to sex. But it is so much more, as we see above. How do you and your husband interact? What is your love language? Do you dance in the rain? Do you dance while cooking dinner? Do you sit close to one another on the couch? Do you hold hands every chance you get?

Do you flirt with each other? Flirt? You might ask, "Why do I have to flirt with my husband and he with me?" Because intimacy is all-encompassing. It shows your spouse you are still interested, and that you still enjoy your spouse and those moments you create. For example, my husband was an auctioneer at an auction recently. He was on stage, and I was there supporting him (also a sign of intimacy). I was getting him some water because he was sick that weekend to the point of fever and loss of his voice. He was struggling to get the words out, coughing, and horse, yet striving on to fulfill the task at hand. As I was heading back to our table, I had to pass right in front of the stage. I looked over in his direction, and he looked my way, our eyes locked briefly, and he winked at me. Needless to say, my heart skipped a beat, and my stomach did a flip-flop, bringing me back to when we were dating, as he would wink at me from across the room frequently. Very few people, if anyone, caught this moment between us. But it was one of love, flirtation, and intimacy. I share this to let you know that even the smallest gesture has a great impact.

Once we are able to connect on a flirtatious, service oriented, honesty induced, compassion filled, time spent, forgiveness giving, and life honoring level, we can then move onto sexual intimacy. As this is a very important aspect in your marriage, one where you become one flesh with the other on a level meant for just the two of you. It is a gift from our Heavenly Father.

What is the purpose of Sex:

<u>Making babies</u>
"God blessed them and said to them,
"Be fruitful and increase in number;
fill the earth and subdue it. Rule over the fish in
the sea and the birds in the sky and over every
living creature that moves on the ground."
Genesis 1:28 (NIV)

<u>Intimacy</u>
He
"How beautiful you are, my darling! Oh, how beautiful!
Your eyes are doves."

She
How handsome you are, my beloved!
Oh, how charming!
And our bed is verdant."
Song of Songs 1:15-16 (NIV)

"My beloved spoke and said to me,

"Arise, my darling,
My beautiful one, come with me"
Song of Songs 2:10 (NIV)

"My beloved is radiant and ruddy,
outstanding among ten thousand."
Song of Songs 5:10 (NIV)

<u>Pleasure</u>
"Let him kiss me with the kisses of his mouth—
for your love is more delightful than wine."
Song of Songs 1:2 (NIV)

"My beloved is to me a sachet of myrrh resting
between my breasts."
Song of Songs 1:13 (NIV)

"Like an apple tree among the trees of the forest,
So is my beloved among the young men. In his shade
I took great delight and sat down, and his
fruit was sweet to my taste."
Song of Songs 2:3 (NLT)

Song of Songs or Song of Solomon, one in the same, is a powerful portrait of how intimacy and pleasure can be found in your sexual relationship with your husband. As a challenge to you, read through Song of Songs with your husband and try not to blush.

We see where sexual intimacy is more than pleasure and closeness. There is another aspect to this side of your relationship as well. It can be sex, that is, a way of healing in your relationship. An argument broke out, a divide was created either by you or your husband, actions were taken, and words were said that you/he might regret. So, you come back together in time, when ready to repair and mend the brokenness. Don't get me wrong, this is not a quick "fix" to life's problems. But it is a healing aspect to reconnect in such a way that brings about a peace within your soul that was divided

Corinthians 7:5 (NLT) says, *"Do not deprive each other of sexual relations, unless you both agree to refrain from sexual intimacy for a limited time so you can give yourselves more completely to prayer. Afterward you should come together again so that Satan won't be able to tempt you because lack of self control"*.

Prayer

Dear Lord,

  Intimacy is far greater than just sex. I ask You Lord that you would show both my husband and I what true intimacy looks like. Scriptural intimacy. Not what the world tells us, but what You show us. To have a love like no other for You and for each other. To come together as one flesh. Creating a safe place for one another so we can get lost in each other. So we can get lost in You. I ask that we would be able to read through Song of Solomon and take hold of the truths and the intimacy it shows for a husband and wife. That we can get lost in one another, take pleasure in one another and trust one another on a whole new level. I praise you Lord in Your name, I pray. Amen

Notes

My Prayer

Day 25
Wife – Serve

"For even the Son of Man did not come to be served, but to serve,"
Mark 10:45a (NIV)

Serve - but not slave

We see Jesus humble Himself to His disciples in John 13:1-17 by wrapping a towel around His waist, by pouring water into a basin, and by washing and drying their feet. He positioned Himself lower than his disciples and showed them an example of what it looks like to serve one another.

What I find interesting and quite significant aside from Jesus humbling Himself to wash His disciples' feet was the timing in which He did it. Jesus, according to the Scriptures, *"knew that the hour had come for Him to leave this world and go to the Father"* John 13:1. Despite what lay ahead for Jesus, crucifixion on the cross, He still managed to serve those around Him. In His despair, we see when Jesus prayed His prayer to the Lord in the Garden of Gethsemane, *"My soul is overwhelmed with sorrow to the point of death"* Matthew 26:38, He served. He was faithful to His calling. He was faithful to His disciples. He was faithful to you and me. As He washed His disciples' feet, the depth and breadth of its meaning goes far beyond the surface. Jesus says to Peter, *"You do not realize now what I am doing, but later you will understand."* John 13:7. Jesus was ready, willing, and able to serve those around Him. He was willing to humble Himself and to be the example to all of us that even in our moments of deep despair, deep sorrow, where our soul is so overwhelmed to the point of death, we can humble ourselves and serve others.

Does this mean we are to wash our husbands' feet? Perhaps if needed, and if he is in need of a reminder of Jesus and His love for him.

I was having a pretty rough week. You know those types of weeks that just knock you down. One that takes your breath away (and not in a good way). The kind of week where the only strength you have left is to bend your knees in prayer, to keep your eyes and head in the Word, kind of week. I didn't even have the opportunity to shower, shave or even wash my hair, type week. My husband, in the midst of trying to keep his head above water type week himself, taking care of the kids, the business and everything else in between, looks over in my direction, sees the look on my face and says "Baby, jump up on the counter and let me wash your feet." Instead of getting frustrated, instead of looking inward to all the responsibilities that lay ahead of him, he saw in this moment the need to take care of his wife. He helped me up on the counter that day, placed my feet in the sink and washed them for me. He did this all with such grace and love. This spoke volumes to me and it showed me not only how much he loves me but how much he loves the Lord. That he will follow in His footsteps and His example of how to serve those around him.

" Now that I, your Lord and Teacher, have washed your feet, you also should wash one another's feet. I have set you an example that you should do as I have done for you. Very truly I tell you, no servant is greater than his master, nor is a messenger greater than the one who sent him. Now that you know these things, you will be blessed if you do them."
John 13:14-17 (NIV)

In Genesis 2:18 (NIV) *"The Lord God said "It is not good for the man to be alone. I will make a helper suitable for him"*

Matthew Henry said this; "The woman was made of a rib out of the side of Adam; not made out of his head to rule over him, nor made out of his feet to be trampled upon by him, but at his side to be equal with him, under his arm to be protected, and near his heart to be loved by him."

People often ask my husband and I about our business and how I am a part of it. Our answer is almost always that I am his suitable helper, just like the Bible tells us.

My husband has had a lifelong passion for cars, teaching and creating. He goes through life seemingly easy, ideas for products and new developments leap into his head with ease. We like to say they are downloaded straight from God. His life is surrounded by and filled with car talk and car parts. He is constantly thinking and constantly in development mode.

So, what does this mean to me, his wife?

In-depth conversations around cars and different product ideas. People vying for his attention and knowledge. Terminology that I am learning and that I am starting to understand. But life is a constant state of learning and studying, understanding what my husband is passionate about and learning alongside him and for him. I am to study my husband and how he thinks and what makes him, him. For me, it is to come alongside my husband and encourage him daily as he uses his gifts and talents to serve those around him. I support his passion and love for cars, even though l do not have the same passion for cars myself. But instead, I have a passion for my husband. I have a passion to support him in our venture, to build our business around his gifts and his calling. To use my own gifts and talents to fit into and complement his and be able to help strengthen him on our journey.

I am there to uplift, encourage, and support him. That is what it means for me his wife, his suitable helper in all things.

As I am uncovering my own passion, he in turn, is supporting me. He is helping me to grow my own talents and to uplift and compliment me, and to help strengthen me on my journey.

It is a give and take, a back and forth. This, in no way, means that you change who you are. We had an opportunity to start a business and work side by side with each other. Some might not get this kind of opportunity or would even want or benefit from this kind of opportunity, and that is perfectly okay. You need to prayerfully identify where God is calling you to be your husband's suitable helper.

What does this look like for you? In what ways can you be a suitable helper for your husband? Maybe it is something as simple as making his lunch for the next day or a cup of tea at the end of a long day. One great way to figure out what this could look like is to read the Five Love Languages. Figure out how he expresses love, and how he receives love. But don't forget to identify how you express and receive love and make sure you communicate with one another on what these are. This can be a great tool in helping how you interact with one another.

You see, we need to have our eyes up and open to the needs of our spouse, the needs of our children, and the needs of those around us. In the midst of an overwhelmed soul, we can still serve with a heart full of love, of grace, and of peace. To follow the example left by Jesus.

Prayer

Dear Lord,

You created us to serve one another. Not as servants, but as those who love on, and want to take care of each other. I ask that You guide us to Your ways and teach us how we are to better serve one another. Your Word, Lord, teaches us to have humility in the way in which we care for each other. To lift each other up and not to tear each other down. To humbly ask, "What can I do for you today?". Help us be ever present with one another so we will know when the other needs lifted up. As Ecclesiastes 4:9-10 (NIV) says, *"Two are better than one, because they have a good return for their labor, if either of them falls down, one can help the other up"* Give me a love so pure for my husband, and he for me, that we can fully submerge ourselves into this verse and have a good return for our labor. In your precious name, I pray. Amen

Notes

My Prayer

Day 26
Father

"Fathers, do not provoke your children to anger, but bring them up in the disciple and instructions of the Lord"
Ephesians 6:4 (NASB)

Just like being a husband, being a father is of great importance and a very impactful calling, whether or not his child is of blood or of choice. Being a father carries weight and responsibility.

What did your husband love about his own father and what did he dislike? Can he leave in the past what should be left and can he take into the future what should be taken?

Children crave boundaries. They crave consistency, and they crave love. Together, create these areas to be a united front, no back and forth, and no room for the child to gain the "upper hand". Stay strong, stay firm, and stay set in the Scriptures where you reside. Teach your children about the Word, about who God is, His promises to them, and who He says that they are. *"These commandments that I give you today are to be on your hearts. Impress them on your children. Talk about them when you sit at home and when you walk along the road, when you lie down and when you get up."* Deuteronomy 6:6-7 (NIV)

Fathers need to lead by example. Be the man you want your daughter to marry. Be the man you want your son to imitate. And if they wander and stray, remember that you instilled in them God's truth. And know that if you *"Train up a child in the way he should go, even when he is old he will not depart from it"* Proverbs 22:6 (NASB)

We see in the parable of the Prodigal son, a son so consumed by earthly desires, that he asks his father for his inheritance early. His father, who loves him dearly, complies. He grants his son's request and off he goes, inheritance in hand. He lives a life of worldly pleasure, loses all that he has, and now lives a life of despair, one where even the pigs he is caring for have a better life than he. He humbles himself and returns to his father's house, knowing that even if he were to be a servant of his father, his life would be much better than it was in that moment. So, he makes the journey home, and while he was still far off, his father sees him. His father runs to him, gathers him into his arms, and welcomes him home. But what we might miss in all of this is the father. He is watching, and he is waiting for his son to return. Being a man of wealth in this day and age, you wouldn't run; it was unbecoming of a man with his stature. But he lifted his tunic, tucked it into his belt, and he ran. He ran to his son. Not knowing if or when he would return, but being ready if he did. So if your children stray, pray. Be watchful, be diligent and like the father, run to them with arms open wide when they do return. Showing them the love of their father, without shame and without fault. But with love and joy for their return.

How should a father present himself to his children?

Provide for their needs: Spiritually and financially:
"Anyone who does not provide for their relatives, and especially for their own household, has denied the faith and is worse than an unbeliever."
1 Timothy 5:8 (NIV)

"All Scripture is God-breathed and is useful for teaching, rebuking, correcting and training in righteousness,"
2 Timothy 3:16 (NIV)

Manage his household:
"For if a man cannot manage his own household, how can he take care of God's church?"
1 Timothy 3:5 (NLT)

<u>Self-controlled:</u>
"Similarly, encourage the young men to be self-controlled."
Titus 2:6 (NIV)

He has to be a parent first and a friend second. There will be times along the way where they won't like you, and where they will be unhappy with you. But stand firm and stand strong because friendship will more than likely follow.

"Be shepherds of God's flock that is under your care, watching over them—not because you must, but because you are willing, as God wants you to be; not pursuing dishonest gain, but eager to serve; not lording it over those entrusted to you, but being examples to the flock."
1 Peter 5:2-3 (NIV)

He needs to be gentle, yet firm. When disciplining your children, let them know who is in charge. Just don't break their spirit. Children crave and want structure and boundaries.

"No discipline seems pleasant at the time, but painful. Later on, however, it produces a harvest of righteousness and peace for those who have been trained by it."
Hebrews 12:11 (NIV)

"Discipline your children, and they will give you peace; they will bring you the delights you desire."
Proverbs 29:17 (NIV)

Don't be harsh with them:

"Fathers, do not provoke your children, lest they become discouraged."
Colossians 3:21 (NKJV)

"As a father shows compassion to his children, so the Lord has compassion on those who fear him."
Psalm 103:13 (NIV)

He needs to spend time with them. Quality time. Make sure you have family night, "date" night and Bible study night. We already see this instructed in Deuteronomy 6:6-7, but when the Bible repeats itself, we need to listen. So, it bears repeating here.

> *"You shall teach them to your children, talking about them when you sit at home and when you walk along the road, when you lie down, and when you get up."*
> Deuteronomy 11:19 (NIV)

He needs to pay attention. If he is busy and your children have something to say or something to show, take the time. If your daughter wants to dance, dance. If your son wants to throw a ball, throw the ball. Be there, be present. They want you more than what you can give them, materialistically or financially. What you are working on will still be there. But they will only be this age (whatever age they may be) for a short period of time. It is fleeting and goes by oh so very fast.

> *"Children are a heritage from the Lord, offspring a reward from him."*
> Psalm 127:3 (NIV)

He needs to allow for mistakes from them and from you. Ask forgiveness where forgiveness needs to be asked in whatever way that speaks to them.

> *"Be kind and compassionate to one another, forgiving each other, just as in Christ God forgave you."*
> Ephesians 4:32 (NIV)

When a child is a child, they are childish, but should not be foolish. As a parent, you need to discern between the two.

> *"When I was a child, I spoke and thought and reasoned as a child. But when I grew up, I put away childish things."*
> 1 Corinthians 13:11 (NLT)

I remember one day I got in an argument with my daughter. If you were to ask me now what it was about, I would tell you I do not recall.

What I do recall is that I was in the wrong. I messed up, and I jumped to conclusions that were not right. Both of us were upset. She went to her room crying and not speaking to me. I sat there for a time mulling over the conversation, realizing my fault in the matter. I gathered my things, and I walked out of the house and down to the store. There, I bought her favorite thing for her. Bacon. When I got home, I made up the bacon, and I arranged it on a cookie sheet to say I'm sorry. It was a small gesture. That meant a lot. Don't be so afraid to say I'm sorry, especially if you are in the wrong. It will speak volumes to your children, and it will teach them the art of forgiveness.

Being a parent is not for the faint of heart. It comes with many challenges, many heartbreaks, but many many rewards and tremendous amounts of love, happiness, and joy. And when the time is right, friendship.

Prayer

Dear Lord,

Oh Lord, being a parent is so very hard, yet so very rewarding. I pray that my husband will be the example he needs to be for our children. That they will have a personal relationship with him. That he would be the type of father/man that they want to look up to. One who holds their life so gently in his hands. To not exacerbate them, but to uplift them. To not rule over them with an iron fist, but to lead them in love. And when they do wrong, and they will, I ask that my husband would approach the situation with gentleness, with understanding and with a great amount of calmness and of love. I pray that his relationship with each and everyone of his children be filled with a love so great that they take it into their own marriages and into their own families. The example of what it looks like to be a husband and a father. Help my husband be who You have called him to be. In Your precious name, I pray. Amen.

Notes

My Prayer

Day 27
Leading his family

*"But I want you to understand that Christ is the head of
every man, and the man is the head of a woman,
and God is the head of Christ"*
1 Corinthians 11:3 (NASB)

"Where you go I will go, and where you stay I will stay" Ruth 1:16 (NIV)

We often reference this verse when talking about marriage. But we see Ruth say this not to her husband, but to Naomi, her mother-in-law. Naomi was wrought with heartache as her husband had passed away, and then shortly thereafter, both of her sons also passed away. So, Naomi in her heartache decides that she will make her way back home. She urges Ruth to return to her own family, but Ruth does not want to part from her mother-in-law whom she grew to love and cultivated a relationship with.

This is such a great imagery for marriage. *"Where you go I will go, where you stay I will stay"* But are you actually willing to go where your husband goes, or stay where he stays? When you feel a bit nervous, a bit apprehensive about where the call on his heart is taking you. Are you willing when where you are at is comfortable, is "safe", is known, but where you would be going brings about so much possibility and potential to further God's Kingdom? It can be scary to give up the known, the comfortable, the "safe", and walk into the unknown.

Our husbands have a call on their lives to lead our families. There is an order of operations, a process here, and an example to follow of who to follow. In 1 Corinthians 11:3, we see this. Here, we get an understanding of how this all works. It doesn't start off with the husband being the head of the wife. It starts off with Christ being the head of every man, and it flows out from there. Christ is the example for our husbands.

Your husband is called to lead, to step out in responsibility and risk. He must be able to follow Christ's leadership, and he must be able to give himself over to the one who gave it all in order to lead his family well. He has to delve into Christ's teaching, His way of life, and His way of doing things. He has to follow after and listen to the voice and Words of God in his life.

He has an opportunity to lead the one he loves in life and in Christ. You have an opportunity to follow the one you love in life and in Christ. This is a gift that should be treasured, one that is not to be taken lightly. *"For the husband is the head of the wife even as Christ is the head of the church, His body, of which He is the savior"* Ephesians 5:23 (NIV) This does not mean your husband leads in dominance or fear. It means that he is to follow Christ's example as He led and leads the church.

Deuteronomy 6:6-7 (NKJV) says *"And these words I command you today shall be in your heart. You shall teach them diligently to your children, and shall talk of them when you sit in your house, when you walk by the way, and when you lie down, and when you rise up"* Your husband needs to be the Spiritual leader of your home, leading in prayer, Bible study, and quiet time. Allowing for all of his family to see this prayer life, his quiet time with the Lord. His family needs to witness him being the man that God called him to be, not just in words but in action. *"Be on guard for yourselves and for all the flock, among which the Holy Spirit has made you overseers, to shepherd the church of God which He purchased with His own blood."* Acts 20:28 (NASB)

Remembering all the while that you his wife is equal with him, right at his side, to move forward together to accomplish what God has called you to do. Your husband leading the way, hand held out, guiding, loving, and protecting as you go.

"Where you go I will go, and where you stay I will stay"

Prayer

Dear Lord,

Oh Father, I ask that my husband will follow Your example of how to lead our family.

His obedience first and foremost towards You. That his prayer life is known to our family. Not in a flaunting "look at me" way, but in an act of obedience to lead. By his example will we be able to flourish and grow ourselves. I ask that my husband will not rule with an iron fist, but rather with a heart of love, of peace, of joy and most importantly of You. There is great responsibility on my husband in this area and I pray that he would take it head on, with full abandon and love. That he would train his children up in the way that they should go, because by his example his children will grow. As our children witness his treatment of their mother, I ask that it would be one of great love, and not of great strife which can lead to confusion and actions less than desirable. Create in my husband a heart after You, so he can lead our family well. In Your name, Lord, I pray. Amen.

Notes

My Prayer

Day 28

Job

"The Lord God took the man and put him in the Garden of Eden to work it and take care of it"
Genesis 2:15 (NIV)

What does your husband want to be known for, truly? His job or his work for the Lord? If his priorities are off, seek the Lord and ask Him to help your husband find his path, and his purpose in the Lord. I had a conversation once with a gal who didn't feel like her day to day was a calling from the Lord, that she wasn't "on mission." We can get caught up in a false sense of what "mission" is. I have to be in a foreign country, sell off everything I own, and haul my family halfway across the world to be a missionary. Well, guess what? In your country, in your state, in your town, on your street, in your home, at your job, at your church, and in your local coffee shop, you and your husband are on mission. Our own backyard where God has placed us, where He has planted us, this is our job, and this is our mission. Our "job" that we do for a paycheck is just that because God knows our needs. He knows our situation. He will take care of us. He will guide us, and He will provide for our needs. We just have to put ourselves out there and be willing to work hard and willing to make an impact no matter where we are and no matter if our message is received or not. Because it is not us, it is the message that people reject.

"But remember the Lord your God, for it is He who gives you the ability to produce wealth" Deuteronomy 8:18a (NIV)

"For the message of the cross is foolishness to those who are perishing, but to us who are being saved it is the power of God" 1 Corinthians 1:18 (NIV)

Man was created from the beginning to work and to work hard.

"Whatever you do, work at it with all your heart, as working for the Lord, not for human masters," Colossians 3:23 (NIV)

If your husband goes into a job he hates every day, try to encourage him to be the best that he can be. Encourage him to go in there each and every day, head held high and with God by his side because he doesn't "work" for them, he works for God. And in working for God, he has to show up differently than everyone else. He is not just representing himself, but he is representing the Almighty God, our Heavenly Father, whom we want to make proud of every step we make and in every breath that we take.

I ask that my husband take Godly pride in what he is doing and to be a man on time all the time. I ask him to work to the best of his ability every day but to remember that when he gets home, his job is not over. I ask that he continues to work and help out at home whether it be with the dishes, making dinner, bathing the children, yard work, etc. Remember not to rob your husband of the gift to care for you and your children. This will show up differently for each household, and some days your husband may work an 18-hour shift. On those days, perhaps his contribution to the home will be less. However, on other days, he might work fewer hours, and it would be more. You'll have to find an appropriate balance for your family dynamic. I remember being a young stay at home wife and mother. My "job" was to care for the children, the home, and my husband. So when my husband came home from a long day of work and would do the dishes, or put a load of laundry in, I would get upset. I would get hurt because he would do such a thing because I thought he thought I was not doing a good enough job. But little did I know that in my upset, I was robbing him of the joy of helping me out. My husband knew that I had a long day with the kids and wasn't able to get everything done that I would have hoped. I was robbing my husband of the blessing. This didn't dawn on me until many years later that in my own upset and blurred vision, I was blocking the blessing that my husband had sought for me. We have to be careful to not diminish the help that our husbands extend to us. Be thankful that they are willing after a long day to come home and participate in the family.

Prayer

Dear Lord,

In everything we are to come at it 100%. In marriage, in being a parent, as a friend, and in our job. I ask you Lord that you would help my husband to work hard and diligently. That he would bring it every day to fulfill his duties to his family and to his job. That he would be on time, all the time, that he would show up differently from his co-workers. That he would be able to stand out above the crowd. But help him Lord to not allow what he does, overshadow who he is. His job is important, but it is not the only thing. Help him to not miss out on opportunities to excel at his job, and to be present in his home. I praise you Lord, in Your name I pray. Amen

Notes

My Prayer

Day 29
Finances

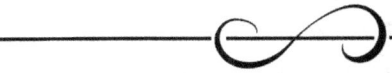

"For where your treasure is, there your heart will be also"
Matthew 6:21 (NKJV)

We sometimes see people who believe that if they are a good person, then God will bless them. If I do this, then God will give me that. They act like God is some kind of cosmic vending machine. Don't get me wrong, I believe that we are blessed for our obedience, but that doesn't always relate to monetary gain. God knows what we need and will provide for us when we need it. Sometimes, we might have to humble ourselves and ask for help, and sometimes a check randomly shows up in the mail that helps reduce the amount of bills you might have piling up. God will at times strip you of the things you are clinging to (maybe even unbeknownst to you) to help you cling and move more closely to Him. To understand that He is our source for everything.

We cannot serve both money and God.

> *"No one can serve two masters, for either he will hate the one and love the other, or he will be devoted to the one and despise the other. You cannot serve God and wealth."*
> Matthew 6:24 (NASB)

We are to be content with what we have.

> *"Keep your lives free from the love of money and be content with what you have, because God has said, "I will never leave you nor forsake you."*
> Hebrews 13:5 (NIV)

> *"For where your treasure is, there your heart will also be"*
> Luke 12:34 (NASB)

> *"For the love of money is a root of all kinds of evil. Some people, eager for money, have wandered from the faith and pierced themselves with many griefs."*
> 1 Timothy 6:10 (NIV)

Now, don't get me wrong, money is needed to get by day to day, month to month, and year by year. And God understands. He knows where you are at. He knows what you need. God will provide. You just have to love God more than you love money.

One area of obedience is tithing. For most, we hear that 10% is where we are to start. But 2 Corinthians 9:7 (NLT) says, *"You must each decide in your heart how much to give. And don't give reluctantly or in response to pressure. "For God loves a person who gives cheerfully."* If 10% is what you can give, awesome. If you can give more, that's great. But if all you can give is less than 10%, and you know in your heart (and you are right with God), then don't stress about it. That is between you and God. But don't fall into the trap of giving less and spending more on worldly things that are not needed. Sometimes, what God is asking of us does not look right on paper, but makes sense and brings peace. And what looks good on paper makes no sense and causes angst and unrest. This is the only area where God says we are allowed to test Him. *"Bring the whole tithe into the storehouse, that there may be food in My house. Test me in this," says the Lord Almighty, "and see if I will not throw open the floodgates of heaven and pour out so much blessing that there will not be room enough to store it."* Malachi 3:10 (NIV)

In our business, we have run the gamut of being in wealth and being in need. Like Paul says in Philippians 4:12-13 (NIV) *"I know what it is to be in need, and I know what it is to have plenty. I have learned the secret of being content in any and every situation, whether well fed or hungry, whether living in plenty or in want. I can do all this through Him who gives me strength."*

I prayed over our business in many areas. I even have a list.

<u>Parking lot - abundance</u>
The Lord will send a blessing on your barns and on everything you put your hand to. The Lord your God will bless you in the land he is giving you."
Deuteronomy 28:8 (NIV)

<u>Front door - grace</u>
"Let us therefore come boldly to the throne of grace, that we may obtain mercy and find grace to help in time of need."
Hebrews 4:16 (NKJV)

<u>Lobby - security</u>
"Then you would trust, because there is hope; And you would look around and rest securely."
Job 11:18 (NASB)

<u>My desk grace and understanding - wisdom and knowledge</u>
"For the Lord gives wisdom; from His mouth come knowledge and understanding"
Proverbs 2:6 (NASB)

<u>Husband's office - peace</u>
"And the peace of God, which surpasses all understanding, will guard your hearts and your minds in Christ Jesus."
Philippians 4:7 (NIV)

<u>Shop - safety</u>
"Discretion will guard you, Understanding will watch over you,"
Proverbs 2:11 (NASB)

<u>Mezzanine</u>
"But remember the Lord your God, for it is he who gives you the ability to produce wealth, and so confirms his covenant, which He swore to your ancestors, as it is today."
Deuteronomy 8:18 (NIV)

<u>Extras</u>
"Commit your works to the Lord and your plans will be established."
Proverbs 16:3 (NASB)

*"and observe what the Lord your God requires:
Walk in obedience to Him, and keep his decrees and commands,
His laws and regulations, as written in the Law of Moses.
Do this so that you may prosper in all you do and wherever you go"*
1 Kings 2:3 (NIV)

The one that stands out the most to me is Deuteronomy 8:18 (NIV) *"But remember the Lord your God, for it is He who gives you the ability to produce wealth, and so confirms His covenant, which He swore to your ancestors, as it is today"* THE. ABILITY. TO. PRODUCE. WEALTH. In other translations, it states that God gives you the power to produce wealth. To me, this means we have to work for it. We have to be willing and able. We cannot just sit back and wait for something to happen, for something to just drop in our laps. God expects participation. He expects us to bring our all, and to be on time, every time, to put forth the maximum amount of effort. To show up in a manner worthy of our calling and to be an example for those around us.

We are also not to hold so tightly to our finances, and to our blessings, because we are blessed to be a blessing.

"You will be enriched in every way so that you can be generous on every occasion, and through us your generosity will result in thanksgiving to God." 2 Corinthians 9:11 (NIV)

Prayer

Dear Lord,

I know in my heart and in my mind that You will provide for our needs. I know that You know exactly where we stand and what our finances look like. I ask for a peace within my husband, and within myself that transcends our bank account. That transcends our daily needs.

Because in all reality You are our greatest and only need. If we focus on You more and focus less on our finances, we find that things will fall into place. That is not to say we become complacent in our work, it just means that we seek You first. I ask that You would give my husband a work ethic like no other, that he would do whatever it takes to provide for his family. Whether he is sick, hurting, tired, frustrated or anything else, that he would be able to put all discomfort aside and work to provide for our needs. I ask that You would give him a heart of service towards his family. In Your name, Lord, I pray. Amen.

Notes

My Prayer

Day 30
Fear

*"The Lord is my light and my Salvation-whom shall I fear?
The Lord is the stronghold of my life - of whom,
shall I be afraid."*
Psalm 27:1 (NIV)

My husband and I used to hike all the time. I had a love hate relationship with our hikes and working out in general. I mean, who doesn't, right!?!

When I was alone in my thoughts, it was as if my mind was competing for space as old memories came flooding back and allowing for new memories to be made. Often, the old memories would win and take hold. This is not to say that new memories were not created. It is more like saying that the new memories did not take precedence during this time. But one thing that happened every time regardless of what my mind was thinking is that God found me right where I was. He showed up in many ways—the sun as it shone on my back as we headed up the trail, and the whisper of the wind or the smallest animal as it crossed my path. The beauty of God's creation is all around. I once read somewhere to go outside and soak in God's beauty and to smell God's perfume. This has stayed with me, and ever since, I have had a greater appreciation for the things around me. From the beauty of a sunset or a flower in bloom, to the magnificent sight as you reach the mountain top you have so eagerly climbed.

During one of our cherished hikes, God found me. As I walked along the trail, I was completely and utterly surprised as this thought came to me:

If I were to sum myself up in one word, what would that be: Afraid!

Yes, afraid. I even surprised myself. Afraid, I thought... Yes, afraid as my mind swirled and what I was afraid of became apparent.

I am afraid of my husband tripping and falling on a rock.

I am afraid of falling down the side of the trail.

I am afraid that our children will not follow closely after You.

I am afraid that I am not being the wife and person You created me to be.

I am afraid…

The list in my head went on and on as we hiked the trail that day. It stayed with me that week as I pondered why and how I did not see this before. I guess I knew. I just couldn't sum up in one word how I felt until that day during our hike.

The following Sunday, I was sitting there in church eagerly taking in what our Pastor was saying. The next thing he said hit me like a ton of bricks.

"Why are you so afraid?"
After all that we have been through, do you still have no faith?

I sat there in utter silence as I pondered this question that seemed directly pointed at me.

Yes, why am I so afraid?

Have I learned nothing in my time spent with Him? I know He is my source of comfort, peace, and joy. Remembering that God is always with me.

I wish that I could tell you from that moment on that I was no longer afraid. But what I can tell you is that I have an even better sense and understanding that our God is with me. God is right beside me regardless of any situation, any trial, or any fear. Knowing that Jesus is there to pick up the pieces.

"So do not fear, for I am with you; do not be dismayed, for I am your God. I will strengthen you and help you; I will uphold you with my righteous right hand!" Isaiah 41:10 (NIV)

If we are not careful, being fearful and afraid can leave you lonely, it can leave you bitter, it can leave you paralyzed and in pain. I sometimes wonder why can't we just trust God in all things all the time. The answer is because we all fall short of the glory of God.

When thoughts arise, and feelings dwell, we must learn to be stronger in those moments. We must not allow the enemy access into our innermost being and remind us of things from the past, or of the present, the what ifs and the to comes.

"For God has not given us a spirit of fear and timidity, but of power, love, and self-discipline." 2 Timothy 1:7 (NLT)

The Spirit of power—the power to say to the enemy of our souls, "Get behind me Satan; you have no place in my heart or in my mind. God gives us the power to let it all go and trust that God has us wrapped in His loving arms and is holding and carrying us through our most difficult of times. And when those times get better, and they will, know that He is still there with His arms open wide for us to return to when we do fear, when we are afraid, or when we are in pain, or when we are feeling lonely. Our Heavenly Father is whom we seek refuge. In those times of weakness, we can say, "I'm sad, and I need you to just hold me and take the fear and pain away. And we can say, "I will trust in you forever and always."

"Come to me, all you who are weary and burdened, and I will give you rest. Take my yoke upon you and learn from me, for I am gentle and humble in heart, and you will find rest for your souls. For my yoke is easy and my burden is light." Matthew 11:28-30 (NIV)

Prayer

Dear Lord,

    I come before you today asking for a heart of trust and faithfulness. A heart that does not fear whatever may come our way. To fully submerge ourselves into who You are and to understand that perfect love, Your love casts out our fear. Your word says *"Do not fear, for I am with you"* Isaiah 41:10 (NIV) Oh Lord just knowing that You are here in our midst helps tremendously, it helps us to place our focus on You and what You provide versus our fears and where they might take us. We love you Lord and praise You in Your name, we pray. Amen

Notes

My Prayer

Day 31
Peace/Hope

"Peace I leave with you; My peace I give to you; not as the world gives do I give to you. Let not your heart be troubled, neither let it be afraid"
John 14:27 (NKJV)

What is it like to have peace in the middle of a peace-less moment? What is it like to have hope in the middle of a hopeless moment? What is it like to have both in the middle of strife, in the middle of trials, smack dab in the middle of conflict?

It's that feeling deep down inside of you that tells you everything will be all right. It's that feeling deep down inside of you that comforts you when all seems lost. It's that feeling deep down inside of you that makes absolutely no sense and does not match up with where you are at or how your emotions are turning around inside of you. It's that still small voice of God our Father letting you know that He is leading you, loving you, and holding you when you feel most fragile and vulnerable.

We see all of this and more played out in front of us in 2 Corinthians 1:1-11 (NASB). Paul is recounting a mission's trip he and Timothy made to the province of Asia. Without mincing words, Paul says that they experienced troubles while they were there. The kind of trouble where they were under great pressure. Paul says that the pressure was *"that we were burdened excessively, beyond our strength, so that we despaired even of life;"* v.8. He goes on to say that they felt like they had received the sentence of death.

Have you ever been in a situation, or a place where the pressures you were under made you feel as if you could not endure, so much so, that you despaired of life itself? The pressure was so thick and heavy you felt like you had just received your own death sentence? With what seems like nowhere to turn? You may ask, "Why God am I here? What God am I to learn from this situation? Where do you want me to go from here, Lord? I don't understand, please help me grasp my here and now and to move into my future." Thoughts and questions surface and more than likely consume your prayer time.

Let's go back to 2 Corinthians 1:1-11. We see Paul's experience sandwiched between the answer right there in black and white. This is what we need to focus on when life gets tough and it seems impossible to breathe.

"Blessed be the God and Father of our Lord Jesus Christ, the Father of mercies and God of all comfort, who comforts us in all our affliction so that we will be able to comfort those who are in any affliction with the comfort with which we ourselves are comforted by God. For just as the sufferings of Christ are ours in abundance, so also our comfort is abundant through Christ. But if we are afflicted, it is for your comfort and salvation; or if we are comforted, it is for your comfort, which is effective in the patient enduring of the same sufferings which we also suffer; and our hope for you is firmly grounded, knowing that as you are sharers of our sufferings, so also you are sharers of our comfort".
2 Corinthians 3:3-7 (NASB)

"indeed, we had the sentence of death within ourselves so that we would not trust in ourselves, but in God who raises the dead; who delivered us from so great a peril of death, and will deliver us, He on whom we have set our hope. And He will yet deliver us," v. 9-10 (NASB)

What do we take away from this? First and foremost, God is a God of all comfort. He meets us right where we are at and in turn, we are to use the comfort that we were given to provide comfort to those around us. We are not to hold on to the gift that God gave to us, but we are to be generous and lovingly share it with others. Second, we are to ask others to pray on our behalf. As we learned from the paraplegic man, sometimes our faith is on loan, and we need those around us to cover us in prayer when we might not have the strength or the words to do so on our own or in the event where we need our friends to stand beside us as we cry and pray together for the good of the situation. Third, we see the hope that God provides in an otherwise hopeless situation. We see them press into God when they thought all hope was lost. They filled themselves with who God was and moved forward into their calling with Him in the middle.

Last, but certainly not least, we see endurance. We see that others also share in the same sufferings. We see that together, knowing we are not alone in our situation, we can come together as a body of Christ and persevere. We can endure and lean on those around us.

Despite our trials and despite our sufferings, we will always have hope, comfort, and peace. Don't forget to look up and don't forget to come to the cross and sit at Jesus' feet. He is willing; He is ready, and He is able. Trust in Him to supply all of your needs. And don't forget, *"Instead, you must worship Christ as Lord of your life. And if someone asks about your hope as a believer, always be ready to explain it."* 1 Peter 3:15 (NLT)

Prayer

Dear Lord,

There is hope and peace in the midst of troubles and of strife. I ask that You would be there in the middle, comforting us as we go through situations that are less than desirable. I pray that we will be able to press into You and surround ourselves with friends who will lift us up. We find our strength in who You are. We know that You will meet us right where we are at. You will hold us, and You will guide us. Your word says that *"You will keep in perfect peace those whose minds are steadfast, because they trust in You"* Isaiah 26:3. I pray for perfect peace, a peace that surpasses all understanding. A peace that only comes from You. I praise You Lord and I worship You. In Your name, I pray. Amen.

Notes

My Prayer

Day 32
Protection

"But let all who take refuge in you be glad, let them ever sing for joy. Spread your protection over them, that those who love your name may rejoice in you"
Psalm 5:11 (NIV)

We see David cry out numerous times in the Psalms for protection to be kept safe from his enemies. David was pursued and wanted dead by many. At one point, he was pursued by his very own son, a son who wanted the throne, and was thirsty for power, attention and greed.

A psalm of David. When he fled from his son Absalom!

Lord, how many are my foes!
How many rise up against me!

Many are saying of me,
"God will not deliver him."

But you, Lord, are a shield around me,
my glory, the One who lifts my head high.

I call out to the Lord,
and he answers me from his holy mountain.

I lie down and sleep;
I wake again, because the Lord sustains me.

I will not fear though tens of thousands
assail me on every side.

Arise, Lord!
Deliver me, my God!
Strike all my enemies on the jaw;
break the teeth of the wicked.

From the Lord comes deliverance.
May your blessing be on your people.
Psalm 3 (NIV)

We will encounter people who want to do us harm. We will encounter people who want no resolution. We will encounter people who are not trustworthy and people who lie to get what they want. So how are we to respond? We use the Scriptures as our guiding light. *"Your word is a lamp to my feet and a light to my path"* Psalm 119:105 (NASB) We look at the Scriptures first and foremost when making a decision and going through trials, even in times of joy. Pray over the situation you are going through. Remember *"When they hurled their insults at Him, He did not retaliate, when He suffered, He made no threats. Instead, He entrusted Himself to Him who judges justly"* 1 Peter 2:23 (NIV)

God promises to protect His children. He promises to be our stronghold in days of trouble. I have this recurring dream. I am in a store, a mini mart of sorts, in the back by the cold cases. In walks a man, ready, willing and able to rob the place and to take out anyone who gets in his way—a man set on vengeance. I duck down and try to hide, but he finds me, aims his gun in my direction and fires. In my panic, I find peace. In my panic, I find myself being calm. I start to sing "Amazing Grace, how sweet the sound." As the bullet nears, I lunge out of the line of fire. The bullet slows down, and it drops to the ground. I am safe.

Are we always saved on this earth from those who intend harm? No, but God promises that He will use what was intended for evil for good. *"Do not be afraid of those who kill the body but cannot kill the soul. Rather be afraid of the one who can destroy both soul and body in hell"* Matthew 10:28 (NIV)

God will redeem, He will protect, and He will comfort always. *"We are hard pressed on every side but not crushed; perplexed, but not in*

despair; persecuted, but not abandoned; shut down, but not destroyed"
2 Corinthians 4:8-9 (NIV)

Prayer

Dear Lord,

     Your word says that You are our stronghold in days of trouble. You know us as we take refuge in You and Your promises. Lord You say that those who believe in You will find refuge, those who believe in You will find protection. Those who believe in You will find peace and healing, those who believe will find shelter from the storm. We ask for Your favor, Lord; we ask Your promise; we ask for Your comfort; we ask for Your protection. In Your name, Lord, I pray. Amen

Notes

My Prayer

Day 33
Wife – Respect

"So again I say, each man must love his wife as he loves himself, and the wife must respect her husband."
Ephesians 5:33 (NLT)

Respect - but not disrespected

What does respect really mean? Respect as a verb means to hold in esteem or honor. We are to honor our husbands and their position in our lives. Respect starts with your husband's love for you. He is to love you as himself, and from this flows your respect to him. This again points us to Christ. Our husbands are to love us as Christ loves the church. Jesus is the ultimate example of how we, as wives and our husbands, are to show our love and respect to one another.

So what happens if your husband lacks the love of Christ for you? Are you supposed to still show respect and love for him? The answer, in my opinion, is yes. Your actions and responses flow from your relationship with the Lord. Just like submission, we respect because we are obedient to the Lord.

Now, this does not make you less than, and this does not give up self-respect. Prayerfully, we seek that it does the opposite. 1 Peter 3:1 (NIV) says, *"Wives in the same way submit yourselves to your own husbands so that if any of them do not believe the word, they may be won over without words by the behavior of their wives"*

So regardless of his actions, we are still to love, submit, and respect our husbands. And if they need correction, we are to do this in a manner worthy of our calling. We are to gently and lovingly guide them back to the center of who God is and His commands to our husbands in how they are to interact and love us their wives. As in Colossians 3:19 (NIV), *"Husbands, love your wives and do not be harsh with them."*

Respect in marriage is about talking openly and honestly with one another. It is about intentionally listening to what the other has to say. Engaging with one another. Respect is about valuing the other person, their feelings and their needs.

However, respect also goes beyond the marriage covenant. In 1 Peter 2:17, Peter says, *"Show proper respect to everyone, love the family of believers, fear God, honor the emperor."* Meaning, we show respect to our children, our parents, our co-workers, and our boss. We show respect to our neighbor down the street or the person who you run into at the store. We love and honor all. And we are to respect the governing authorities whether we like them or not. Romans 13 states that the governing authorities were put into place by God Himself. Yes, there might come a time when civil disobedience might be needed if the governing authorities are willfully taking away your rights. But that is a whole other conversation. Most importantly, we are to respect, honor, and love God. Respect is something that is handed down, it is given, and it is shared. Respect is a command from God. Even if you disagree with someone, you can still show respect, love, and peace to them because respect stems from God. And God is an all loving, all knowing, all caring, grace and mercy filled God.

Prayer

Dear Lord,

Oh Lord, I ask that You show us what true respect for one another is and what it looks like. We might think respect has to be earned, or it has to just be given because of who the person is. Both true, but it extends so much deeper. Help us to gently and lovingly move through our marriage, to follow your example of what true Scriptural respect looks like. I ask You Lord that You would give my husband a heart after You. That he would truly, seriously study how to love me, how to respect me and how to treat me as Your Word guides him there.

Guide me in Your ways Lord and give me a love so deep that respect flows through me, because I am so deeply in love with You that my responses and my actions flow from my relationship with You. In Your name, Lord, I pray. Amen.

Notes

My Prayer

Day 34
Integrity

"The integrity of the upright will guide them, but the crookedness of the treacherous will destroy them"
Proverbs 11:3 (NASB)

Integrity: The quality of being honest and having strong moral principles; moral uprightness.

Ananias and Sapphira are husband and wife. We read their story in Acts 5:1-11 (NIV).

Because of their lack of integrity, they lost their lives. Let me explain. Ananias and his wife Sapphira owned some land together. They sold their land, both knowing full well the entire amount that they received from selling their land. First, we see Ananias bring his "proceeds" before Peter. Peter, knowing that Ananias was not telling the truth about how much money he and his wife had received, confronts Ananias, and the Scriptures say that after hearing this he fell down and died.

Three hours later, his wife Sapphira comes in. Peter asks her one simple question, *"Tell me, is this the price you and Ananias got for the land?"* Boldly, she proclaims, "Yes" she said "that is the price" v.8 when we all know, including Peter, that she was lying. Back in verse 2 we are told *"With his wife's full knowledge he kept back part of the money for himself but brought the rest and put it at the apostles' feet."* We then see Sapphira fall down at Peter's feet and die.

Now, let me go back a bit further to Acts 4:32-35. (NIV) Here we see it explained why this was such an issue, one maybe not worthy of death, but who they lied to and "stole" from certainly was worthy of death.

The believers shared their possessions, *"All the believers were one in heart and mind. No one claimed that any of their possessions was their own, but they shared everything they had. With great power the apostles continued to testify to the resurrection of the Lord Jesus. And God's grace was so powerfully at work in them all. For from time to time those who owned land or houses sold them, brought the money from the sales and put them at the apostles' feet, and it was distributed to anyone who had need"*

The stage was set, the need known, and the promises made. With money from these sales, the apostles were able to continue on with their ministry. They were also able to use the money needed to minister to those in need.

Ananias and Sapphira both knew and understood, and both agreed to willingly give whatever profit was gained from the sale of their land, just as the other believers who were all in this tight-knit group together did.

Their hearts were not right. They were not living in integrity with each other, with their group, and with the apostles, but most importantly, with God. They were selfish and greedy, seeking the "attention" of others for how good this made them look. They were posturing themselves to be better than they were.

Peter was not concerned with himself, the apostles, or their followers, for he knew God held them closely and would take care of them. His concern was the Lord *"How could you conspire to test the Spirit of the Lord?"* v.9

God sees. God knows. He knows if you are living up to how you are supposed to live, how you said you would live, and the promises you have made to yourself, to others, and to God Himself. *"Would not God find this out? For He knows the secrets of the heart"* Psalm 44:21 (NASB)

Prayer

Dear Lord,

    Oh Lord, You know the secrets of our hearts. I ask that You would uncover, in my husband and myself, areas that we might not be living up to who we said we were. That we would live in integrity, being honest, loyal, and obedient. If there is any area that needs work, Lord I ask that You would show us. As we want to live a life that is pleasing to You. A life that shines Your light to those around us. We shouldn't be doing things to posture ourselves to others, it is about You Lord and what You have done in our lives and through our lives. In Your name, I pray. Amen.

Notes

My Prayer

Day 35
Words/Speech

"A soft answer turns away wrath, but a harsh word stirs up anger"
Proverbs 15:1 (NKJV)

The words you choose to speak are so very important. They can either lift a person up or tear them down. *"The tongue has the power of life and death, and those who love it will eat its fruit"* Proverbs 18:21 (NIV). Immediately following this is verse 22 *"He who finds a wife finds what is good and receives favor from the Lord"* (NIV). Every word within the Scriptures is perfectly placed with intention and meaning. So, I do not think this verse was placed here on accident. I think it was placed there to reinforce the power of a husband's words towards his wife. Husbands are to be considerate as they live with their wives. They are to treat them with respect as the weaker partner. Peter 3:7a, but it doesn't stop there. Husbands are to live with their wives *"as heirs with you of the gracious gift of life, so that nothing will hinder your prayers"* 1 Peter 3:7b (NIV)

It is so imperative of how a husband treats and interacts with his wife because his prayers to the Lord depend on it. Did you catch that…? Your husband's prayers depend on, and can be hindered, if he is unkind and mistreats his wife.

Are your words helping or hurting? Are they uplifting or deflating? Do they make your husband feel better or worse? Are the words of your husband helping or hurting? Are they uplifting or deflating? Do they make you feel better or worse? We have to be careful of the words we choose to speak, as we will have to give an account for every careless word that we speak.

<u>We are instructed to speak as though our words are seasoned with salt</u>
*"Let your conversation be always full of grace, seasoned
with salt, so that you may know how to answer everyone."*
Colossians 4:6 (NIV),

When you add salt to something sweet, it becomes sweeter, and that is why people add salt on cantaloupe, in cookies, or even on watermelon.

<u>Be slow to speak</u>
*"My dear brothers and sisters, take note of this:
Everyone should be quick to listen, slow to speak and
slow to become angry, because human anger does not
produce the righteousness that God desires."*
James 1:19-20 (NIV).

<u>Listen before answering</u>
"To answer before listening—that is folly and shame."
Proverbs 18:13 (NIV).

<u>Do not be hasty with our words</u>
*"Do you see someone who speaks in haste? There is
more hope for a fool than for them."*
Proverbs 29:20 (NIV).

For a gentle answer turns away wrath
*"A gentle answer turns away wrath, but a
harsh word stirs up anger."*
Proverbs 15:1 (NIV).

<u>Our words and those of our husbands should be sweet to the soul and healing to the bones</u>
*"Gracious words are a honeycomb, sweet to the soul
and healing to the bones"*
Proverbs 16:24 (NIV)

Wow, healing to the bones... Take a minute and let this one sink in... The words you speak go deep into the soul of a person. As the bones are the depth of the body, so is the soul the depth of the person.

<u>We will have to give account for every word spoken</u>
"But I tell you that every careless word that people speak, they shall give an accounting for it in the day of judgment."
Matthew 12:36 (NASB)

Our words hold weight. Our husband's words hold weight. Pray over your husband's words of affirmation, words of healing, and words that are sweet. And pray for your husband's words towards you, your children, his family, and his friends.

"He who restrains his words has knowledge. And he who has a cool spirit is a man of understanding" Proverbs 17:27 (NASB)

Prayer

Dear Lord,

Our words hold so much power, I ask that my husband's words would be sweet, that they would be filled with affirmation and be uplifting. Not words that tear me down. And in turn Lord, I ask the same of myself, that my words would be filled with affirmation and be uplifting. That as we speak to one another, each word would be chosen, each word would be perfectly matched to the conversation at hand. I ask that we would think before we speak. As my daughter says, "Are you helping or hurting?" Lord I ask that we would be helping and not hurting one another. That if fights and disagreements arise, and they will, that we would handle them with grace, mercy, and healing words. In Your name, I pray. Amen

Notes

My Prayer

Day 36
Honesty

"The Lord detests lying lips, but He delights in those who tell the truth"
Proverbs 12:22 (NLT)

"He lacks the smoothness of an experienced liar…"

I actually read this in a forum posted by another commenter after a purchaser tried to steal from a business. Essentially saying, you don't lie well enough to cheat and or steal. It gives us an insight into who some, not all, people are and what they are capable of. To be applauded for speaking falsities, as though lying was to be admired and looked up to, or somehow a skill that needed to be developed. Society is encouraging people into thinking it is all right, or justifiable, to mislead others with their lies. This makes them think if they lie well enough, or long enough, they can get what they want, at least from an earthly perspective.

They are turning what is good to evil and what is evil to good. *"Woe to those who call evil good and good evil, who put darkness for light and light for darkness, who put bitter for sweet and sweet for bitter."* Isaiah 5:20 (NIV)

Is this really what our world is coming to? Those who look up to and who want to be in community with someone who lies to them? Someone who is being outright dishonest when it comes to relationships, business, the workplace… where does it end? Someone who will cheat the system to gain what they desire regardless of the cost to others?

The world, it seems, is being filled with dishonest people. People who are not afraid to lie for whatever, at whatever cost. It doesn't seem to matter who gets in their way or who they hurt along the way.

As Christians, we need to take another approach. We need to speak words of truth and words of hope and words that uplift and spur others on. As Christians, we are held to a higher standard as we are in the world, but not of the world. We are to view things through the lens of Christ and the example that He has shown us through the Scriptures. *"Don't copy the behavior and customs of this world, but let God transform you into a new person by changing the way you think. Then you will learn to know God's will for you, which is good and pleasing and perfect."* Romans 12:2 (NLT). Not what is earthly or humanly "correct", but what surpasses all of that, what reaches far beyond what we can even comprehend. Life is hard, and being honest is hard, but we are called according to His purpose. As we are not fighting against flesh and blood, we are fighting against those who are against the Lord and His purpose. We are fighting against the evil forces of this dark world that has been broken by our own rebellion and has fallen. We call upon the name of the Lord to combat evil. We use the Scriptures to teach and to guide us. We are to hold the truth in our hearts and to always seek His will and counsel in the big and the small things.

Is your husband honest in the small things? Pray for your husband's honesty because if he is honest in the small things, he will likely be honest in the big things.

Prayer

Dear Lord,

I pray Lord that my husband will have a heart and mind of honesty. That his first response would not be one of lies. That his heart will be filled with truth, Your truth, and that the overflow of his heart will be of something pure and holy. Lord, I ask that You would guide him in his walk, not only with You, but with his family and others as well. That his work and his home life would be filled with honesty, big or small. In Your name, Lord, I pray. Amen

Notes

My Prayer

Day 37
Trust

"Trust in the LORD with all your heart and lean not on your own understanding"
Proverbs 3:5 (NIV)

How many of us have found ourselves in the middle of a situation, in the middle of a trial, that we could not understand? You could not make it better. Where you just stand there in silence and confusion, wondering how if anything would change.

We find ourselves in Mark 9 (NIV) where we see a father desperate to heal his son. A father willing to go to the depths and not give up. He first goes to some of Jesus' disciples, but they were unable to cast out the demon that had been possessing his son. Once Jesus approached the crowd, they ran to Him and greeted Him. Amongst those in the crowd we find the father. In the father's desperation, he moves quickly to get to Jesus, and the father explains to Jesus what his situation is and that the disciples could not cast out the demon. Jesus' response is in classic Jesus' style. *"You unbelieving generation," Jesus replied, "how long shall I stay with you? How long shall I put up with you? Bring the boy to me."* The father brings Jesus his son, and they discuss how long it had been happening and what occurs when it does. The father asks Jesus, *"But if you can do anything, take pity on us and help us" "If you can'?" said Jesus. "Everything is possible for one who believes"* I didn't quite understand Jesus' response, but after reading other translations, it became clear, the NLT says *"What do you mean, if I can?" Jesus asked.*

Jesus questions the father's faith. He questions whether the father actually believes that Jesus can do what he is asking Him to do. The father responds, *"I do believe; help my unbelief..."* (NASB) I have prayed this very prayer myself; I do believe, help my unbelief. This is not saying that I don't have faith, or that the father didn't have faith, it just means that the last remaining bit needs reassurance, it needs confidence, and it needs Jesus to take us by the hand and tell us, *"All things are possible to him who believes."* (NASB) When it comes to faith, all we need to start out with is so tiny, so small, in fact Jesus relates it to the smallest seed that grows into something far larger than where it started. *"Truly I tell you, if you have faith as small as a mustard seed, you can say to this mountain, 'Move from here to there,' and it will move. Nothing will be impossible for you."* Matthew 17:20 (NIV) The mountains that Jesus talks about here could very possibly be obstacles in your way, challenges that you are facing. But with the strength and power of God, we can do anything as long as we believe and have faith the size of mustard seed.

Afterward, when Jesus was alone in the house with His disciples, they asked Him, *"Why couldn't we cast out that evil spirit?"* Jesus replied, *"This kind can be cast out only by prayer"* (NLT).

Why couldn't the disciples cast out the demon? They were followers of Christ; He gave them the ability and power to do so. I think maybe they lacked the same thing the father lacked, and that was the complete faith that it could actually be done. I am sure that we have all stood in this space a time or two. Can God really do what I am asking? Can He really heal this illness? Can He really strengthen and repair my marriage? Can He bring my children back to the heart of worship and follow after Him? Can He? Will He? The questions are endless. But as we trust in Him, our faith grows and becomes far larger than we ever thought possible. God has placed a helper within us, some translations say an advocate to help us, the Spirit of truth, the Holy Spirit. He will guide us in our journey, and He will give us the strength needed to press forward when times are tough. *"But the Advocate, the Holy Spirit, whom the Father will send in my name, will teach you all things and will remind you of everything I have said to you. Peace I leave with you; my peace I give you. I do not give to you as the world gives. Do not let you hearts be troubled and do not be afraid."* John 14:26-27 (NIV)

I do believe; help my unbelief.

Prayer

Dear Lord,

I do believe; help my unbelief. Just like the father in Mark 9, there are times in my life and the life of my husband that needs some reassurance. Reassurance that You are there.

Reassurance that You care. Reassurance that the truths we read in Your word will come true and will happen. So many questions, so many requests, to just trust in You, in Your word. I pray for complete and utter trust in who You are, and in what Your promises tell me. You, Lord, are the one whom all things flow, whom I can lean on in ALL things ALL the time. In Your name, I pray. Amen

Notes

My Prayer

Day 38
Priorities

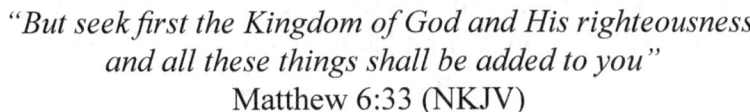

"But seek first the Kingdom of God and His righteousness and all these things shall be added to you"
Matthew 6:33 (NKJV)

I want to look at the story of Mary and Martha found in Luke 10:38-42 (NASB).

"Now as they were traveling along, He entered a village; and a woman named Martha welcomed Him into her home. She had a sister called Mary, who was seated at the Lord's feet, listening to His word. But Martha was distracted with all her preparations; and she came up to Him and said, "Lord, do You not care that my sister has left me to do all the serving alone? Then tell her to help me." But the Lord answered and said to her, "Martha, Martha, you are worried and bothered about so many things; but only one thing is necessary, for Mary has chosen the good part, which shall not be taken away from her."

Martha was anxious and troubled by many things. She was concerned about the cleaning, about what they were going to eat, and about her sister's actions. I am sure we have all been there a time or two. Martha was distracted the Scriptures say. She wanted everything to be just perfect for Jesus. She comes to Jesus as if to tattle on her sister. Whining almost, "Lord, don't you care that my sister has left me to do the work by myself? Tell her to help me!" Note the exclamation mark, there was an emphasis on what she was saying, this just wasn't a small simple polite request. Let's also remember that Jesus was a dear friend of Mary, Martha, and their brother Lazarus. So she probably felt very comfortable with how she was speaking to Jesus. Think about when you are with your really good friends and how conversation flows easy. I know how I can get when Thanksgiving rolls around, or any occasion for that matter. I want everything to be just so, the table set so beautifully, the food prepared and presented just right to create and set the atmosphere for the night. My husband can attest to this, in fact he loves to tell the story of when I was trying to find and buy strawberries for our daughters baby shower. You see, everywhere we went the strawberries were rotten, mold growing, squishy mess. Every carton, as I pulled them off the shelf, bad…. I was frustrated by this and perhaps I placed them back into their places with a little more force than what was necessary, along with an audible mumbling on just how bad they were. This just for my family and friends. Oh man, could you imagine if you got word that Jesus Himself was showing up, how perfect you would want it just for Him. Now don't get me wrong there is nothing wrong with having everything just so, having everything prepared in advance for His arrival. We must be prepared for His coming, to be on guard, to stay awake, to watch and to listen. But where the problem lies within, Martha was in her distraction once Jesus arrived. She was focusing on things that had little bearing to the night, had little bearing to her relationship with our Lord. You see, God looks at the heart. He sees where you are at in any given moment.

The story continues with Jesus telling Martha *"but only one thing is necessary, for Mary has chosen the good part, which shall not be taken away from her"* You see Mary was sitting at the feet of Jesus. She was listening, taking in every word that Jesus said. Soaking in His visit as they were few and far between. She didn't want to miss anything. She was eager to learn, she was eager to hear. Jesus lovingly corrected Martha. Saying *"Martha, Martha," the Lord answered, "you are worried and upset about many things, but few things are needed - or indeed only one."* I imagine Jesus grabbing Martha by the hand, placing His on top of hers and saying *"but only one thing is necessary, for Mary has chosen the good part, which shall not be taken away from her"* He then proceeds to guide Martha around Him to the front of where He is sitting and gently places her at His feet.

The word necessary is what gives me pause. It is so often overlooked but so imperative to the point Jesus is making. If you look at what necessary means you will find the following: required to be done, needed, essential, the basic requirements of life. So with one word this tells me, along with my own experiences, that being in the Word daily, having a relationship with God is essential. It is so essential that it is up there with the basic requirements of life, such as food and water. In John 4:14 (NASB) Jesus says, *"but whoever drinks of the water that I will give him shall never thirst; but the water that I will give him will become in him a well of water springing up to eternal life."* Jesus is saying if you follow Me, if you hear My Word, not just with your ears but with your heart, if you write My Word on the tablet of your heart you will find true peace, your search will be over because the water, His Word, that He gives, will create in you a well to draw from. In good times and in bad. If we continue to draw from God's Word our well will not dry up. It will spring forth our faith in Him, it will spring forth our hope in Him. It will spring forth our eternal life in Him.

Don't get so caught up in the preparation and the "service" that you forget to sit at the feet of Jesus and soak in everything He is saying. Let's not forget to spend time with Him.

My phone is filled with notes of my thoughts. Thoughts of things that have happened, thoughts of encouragement, thoughts of who Jesus is. Things that I want to keep personal and things that I feel led to share. A while ago I was struggling to have these thoughts come to me. Normally they start flooding in the moment my head hits the pillow and I need to write them down before I forget. There are times during the day where I just have to stop what I am doing and jot something down. However, I went through a period of time where I really struggled to find the words. I was disappointed that they were not finding their way to the page, so I prayed about this on a number of occasions. Talking with God I told Him "I don't understand why I cannot find the words, I want to encourage others by what You lay on my heart" and in response God said "You can't be an encourager of the Word if you are not in the Word" Whoa!!! Can I say convicted much!?! Let me say that again. "You can't be an encourager of the Word if you are not in the Word". I am going to be completely honest with you, You see I went a number of days, dare I say weeks, where I did not open a devotional, my Bible study app, or even my Bible (except at church). I used all the typical excuses like, I am so busy with the business, I am not sleeping well, I will do it later, but later never came.

You see, as my time with God dwindled, my well was starting to dry up. I was not drawing on God's Word. I was not sitting at the feet of Jesus. I wasn't drawing from the water that Jesus had offered me. Hebrews 4:12 *"For the Word of God is alive and active. Sharper than any double-edged sword, it penetrates even to dividing soul and spirit, joints and marrow; it judges the thoughts and attitudes of the heart"* God knew the thoughts and attitude of my heart. God's gentle reminder that I need, that we all need, to join Him every day is crucial to our walk together. We need to carve out time to spend with Him. Just like any relationship, time is imperative for it to grow. The beautiful thing about all of this is how gently God corrected me, how He placed His hands on my mine, guided me around, and gently placed me at His feet where I needed to be. We are to surrender, yield and submit to Him every moment of every day.

What does this look like? How am I to have intimacy with God? How am I to surrender, yield and submit to Him? By spending time with Him. Carve out time with the Lord, every day. Figure out what works best for you. In the morning, mid-day, in the evening. Where is your spot you love to be? For me, I love our office. But I need to set this up to be more conducive to using this space daily. I love to hand write out thoughts, or notes, verses. Keep handy paper, pens, pencils if you prefer. Or if you are more of a computer person, make sure that all distractions that come with that are gone. And for you busy moms who think this is all but impossible, get a Bible app, they have a daily verse. Start there each morning. Talk to God while doing dishes, folding laundry, speak truth over your kids while playing with them. As they get older, it will get easier. Listen to worship music and sing at the top of your lungs and dance with your babies. God just wants you. He wants time spent with you. Whatever that might look like for you. You will know if you have been spending enough time with Him. You will know if your husband has been spending enough time with Him. If you are drawing on God's Word your well will spring forth. If you do not draw from the water that Jesus offered you your well will start to dry up. So let's remember that if we want to be an encourager of the Word, we need to be in the Word.

Prayer

Dear Lord,

    I pray for my husband to have the right priorities in life. That You, above all else, would hold his attention. That he would be in Your Word daily, that what he learns and what he reads he can then flow down to his family and his friends. I then ask that his next priority would be his family. That he would want to spend time with us, with me. That he would not prefer to be elsewhere. And if this is currently where his heart is at, I ask that You would grab hold of it and help him see that his family unit is important and that he needs to be shepherding it more.

    With a heart for You, Lord, I ask that he would see and understand the importance of spending time with us and with You. In Your name, Lord, I pray. Amen.

Notes

My Prayer

Day 39
Attitude

"Do everything without grumbling or arguing, so that you may become blameless and pure, "children of God without fault in a warped and crooked generation." Then you will shine among them like stars in the sky"
Philippians 2:14-15 (NIV)

Have you ever had one of those days where it didn't matter what occurred, you were just grumpy? I remember one such day like this. In the midst of God's blessings, my attitude was just not right. I was focusing on all the wrong things. I was being a grumper in my blessings. Have you ever felt this way? Has your husband ever felt this way?

It is an eye opener for sure to sit and be with yourself when you are in a mood like that.

I for one don't like how I feel when I get like that. Do you? Can you imagine how others feel? How your husband feels? We need to reign in our thoughts, our feelings, and our behaviors. How, you ask? Allow yourself 5, maybe 10 minutes to have a pity party. Dwell in, deal with, sort out and move on with whatever has you a grumper in your blessings because no matter the situation, we are to be joyful. *"Rejoice in the Lord always; and again I will say, rejoice!"* Philippians 4:4 (NASB) Another great verse to meditate on (remember filling your mind not emptying it) *"Rejoice always, pray continually, give thanks in all circumstances for this is God's will for you in Christ Jesus"* 1 Thessalonians 5:16-18 (NIV)

Where your heart posture is, your attitude will be. *"for out of the abundance of the heart his mouth speaks"* Luke 6:45b (NKJV)

"Only conduct yourselves in a manner worthy of the gospel of Christ," Philippians 1:27 (NASB). Meaning that whatever the situation, whatever the circumstances, our faith in Jesus is to shine through. We are to hold fast to His example in our lives. Never be hasty with our words. Never be quick to jump to conclusions. Never be quick to enter into an argument. Never be quick to place judgment on someone else. We need to pause and assess the situation, maybe look through it with someone else's lens to see things from their vantage point. We need to stay focused on what really matters and that is grace, mercy, forgiveness, and love. Can you and your husband have these things and maintain a right heart posture through all things?

It won't be easy, but it certainly is easy to try. Keep God's Word hidden in your heart and pull from this when you feel your attitude or the attitude of your husband starts to sway.

Prayer

Dear Lord,

The attitude of the heart is hugely impactful. From the overflow of the heart, the mouth speaks. I pray for an attitude of thankfulness in my husband. I ask that he will be the person You have created him to be. One of love, peace, patience and self-control. Bless him in his walk day to day. Help him achieve a right attitude towards You and towards me. I thank you Lord for the ability to intercede on his behalf. As the saying goes, help him have an attitude of gratitude. In your name, Lord, I pray. Amen

Notes

My Prayer

Day 40

Temptations

"No temptation has overtaken you except what is common to mankind. And God is faithful; He will not let you be tempted beyond what you can bear. But when you are tempted, He will also provide a way out so that you can endure it"
1 Corinthians 10:13 (NIV)

    I read an article once that stated that we as women, we as wives, have the power to keep our husbands from temptations all by making sure that his sexual needs are fulfilled by you and you alone. And if you loved him, you would want to protect him from temptation that surrounds him every day. It basically said that our husbands temptations are under our control, and we can use our "powers" as his wife, as a woman, to stop them.

    Please let me reassure you, and please hear me when I say, that they are completely and 100% wrong. James 1:14-15 (NIV) says *"but each person is tempted and dragged away by their own evil desire and enticed. Then, after desire has conceived, it gives birth to sin and sin, when it is full-grown, gives birth to death"*

Let's break this down:

- But each person - an individual on their own
- Dragged away: To move something away from something else by pulling it while it is on the ground.
    - This is how our own evil desires give way to enticement and temptation
- Desire has conceived: a strong feeling of wanting to have some-

thing or wishing for something to happen. A strong sexual feeling or appetite
- Desire gives birth to sin
- Sin when full-grown gives birth to death

This is a choice that one makes on their own. As temptation takes root, it leads that person astray. We as wives cannot stop when temptation creeps in, when their eyes stray or linger or even when temptation turns into a full-blown affair.

But, what we can do as wives is pray. Pray for our husbands to withstand temptations. Pray that they will be strong enough to say no when temptations present themselves. Pray that their relationship with the Lord is so strong that they can withstand the fiery arrows of the evil one. Pray they have hidden God's Word in their hearts, and they can pull from this when temptations pass them by. Pray their relationship with the Lord is on solid ground, and His Word will not be blown away at the first sign of a storm. Armed with God's Word, God will provide your husband a way out. In doing so, your husband will be able to identify where he needs to go and have the strength needed to say no to temptation.

There is one more thing we can do as wives along with our husbands and that is to set up guardrails and boundaries. With temptations abounding everywhere and easily accessed in this day and age, it is so imperative to set in place and in motion your guardrails and boundaries. I will just name a few I think are very important, and you and your husband can take this list and expand upon it.

Guardrails/Boundaries:

- Never talk to the opposite sex about issues in your marriage
- Never go out with the opposite sex alone: This means
    - Coffee
    - Meals
    - Car rides
    - Etc.
- When messaging the opposite sex ALWAYS include your spouse
- Never be alone with the opposite sex

- Provide your spouse access to all electronic medias
  - Email
  - Text messaging
  - Apps
  - Etc.

We are all called to guard our hearts and our wellbeing, along with that of our spouse. Even Joseph would not be in Potiphar's house alone with Potiphar's wife. He always made sure that someone else was there. And the day that someone was not there, he fled. Interesting choice of words don't you think? Fled: to run away, as from danger or pursuers, to take flight. To move swiftly; fly; speed. Genesis 39: 1-12 (NASB)

If you are reading this and infidelity has already entered into your marriage, please know that there can be healing and restoration. Please know that God has bigger plans than the sins of your husband, *"And the God of all grace, who called you to His eternal glory in Christ, after you have suffered a little while, will Himself restore you and make you strong, firm and steadfast"* 1 Peter 5:10 (NIV)

David was a man after God's own heart, and he failed hard and miserably from his affair with Bathsheba to the murder of her husband. (2 Samuel 11). But when confronted, David was anguished by his actions (convicted) David confessed, but he also had to face the consequences of his sins. (2 Samuel 12:1-22)

Even a man after God's own heart sinned and failed when faced with temptation. But, we see his heart posture change, and we see the grief that was deep inside of him. *"Godly sorrow brings repentance that leads to salvation and leaves no regret, but worldly sorrow brings death"* 2 Corinthians 7:10 (NIV). God is faithful and He can restore what is broken.

Pray for a heart of David for your husband—one of forgiveness, repentance and love.

Remember that your husband (some not all) are grieving a Godly sorrow, and we need to come alongside them to cover them in love, in grace, in mercy, in forgiveness, and in comfort. *"Now instead you ought to*

forgive and comfort him so that he will not be overwhelmed by excessive sorrow. I urge you therefore, to reaffirm your love for him"
2 Corinthians 2:7-8 (NIV)

So, what do I do if my husband does not have a Godly sorrow, if he is not repentant, and does not seek forgiveness?

You immerse yourself in the Scriptures, and surround yourself with Godly people who will pray along with you over your husband. And if your husband dismisses and rejects the call of God on his life, you have a conversation with the Lord.

We know that God hates divorce (Malachi 2:16) but we also know that God understands and is compassionate to His children. He will release you if an unbelieving spouse walks away (1 Corinthians 7:15) or when adultery enters the marriage (Matthew 5:32 and Matthew 19:9). However, remember that God's heart is a heart of reconciliation over separation. Even in times such as these, we are called to pray for and love on, so don't just pray to like your husband, pray to love him continuing to live with him in kindness, gentleness, and self-control.

Circumstances such as these are hard, and should not to be considered lightly. And if, and only if, you have exhausted everything else, and your husband is still showing an unforgiving, unrepentant heart, God can gently release you. This does not come without much prayer, Godly counsel, insight, discernment, and advice, not to mention long talks with the Lord Himself. He will let you know which direction you should move forward in. As you prayerfully consider and way your options, remember this *"If possible, so far as it depends on you, be at peace with all men"* Romans 12:18 (NASB)

Prayer

Dear Lord,

Oh, Lord, I come to you today with a heart after You. I ask You Lord that You would put a barrier up against temptation for my husband.

That he would not fall prey to the enemy or his schemes. That he would be able to stand firm in his beliefs and in his commitment to me, his wife. Lord if temptation has entered and my husband has fallen, I pray that there would be healing, not just healing, but complete healing, complete restoration and complete repentance. Be with us today, Lord God, help us be who you want us to be. I pray for a strong and healthy marriage, that I would not keep any records of wrongs, but rather a heart filled with who You are. I ask that we would be able to set up proper boundaries and guidelines that we both will follow and that temptation will run screaming out of the room. I pray that we will both guard our hearts with Your Word, Lord, that we would write them on the tablets of our hearts. In your precious name, Lord, I pray. Amen

Notes

My Prayer